THE MAGIC OF
MARIE
LAVEAU

...

Embracing the Spiritual Legacy of
The Voodoo Queen
of New Orleans

DENISE ALVARADO

FOREWORD BY CAROLYN MORROW LONG

WEISER
BOOKS

This edition first published in 2020 by Weiser Books, an imprint of Red Wheel/Weiser, LLC
With offices at:
65 Parker Street, Suite 7
Newburyport, MA 01950
www.redwheelweiser.com

Copyright © 2020 by Denise Alvarado
Foreword © 2020 by Carolyn Morrow Long

ISBN: 978-1-57863-673-0

Library of Congress Cataloging-in-Publication Data available upon request.
Cover photograph © 2013, 2020 Matthew Dickstein
Typeset in ITC Berkeley Old Style

Printed in Canada
MAR
10 9 8 7 6 5 4

Any herbal remedies provided in this book have not been evaluated by
the United States Food and Drug Administration and are not approved to
diagnose, treat, cure, or prevent disease. Use due diligence if replicating
any of the activities described herein.

from reading *The Magic of Marie Laveau* and believe this book will become definitive in the continually growing legacy of the greatest Voodoo Queen of New Orleans. A must-have for your collection and a truly wonderful read."
—Witchdoctor Utu, author of *Conjuring Harriet "Mama Moses" Tubman and the Spirits of the Underground Railroad*

"New Orleans Voodoo has a tradition of strong women practitioners. To have one such strong practitioner writing about another is not only a pleasure, it is most proper and most appropriate. *The Magic of Marie Laveau*'s three parts move effortlessly from history to practice to legacy. With sure strokes, Denise Alvarado draws together the past, present, and future creating a literary veve imbued with honor and respect for the great Marie Laveau. Ours is a growing tradition, and this work combines both accurate information and inspiration to provide sure ground for such growth.

"'Becoming a Devotee,' the second part of this book, speaks directly to the present growth of New Orleans Voodoo. The homeless, the sick, and the poor are not forgotten by Denise in this section, as they were not forgotten by Marie in her practices. Marie Laveau's actions toward society's most vulnerable is as a valuable guide to devotees. Alvarado does not portray Laveau as embodying an unattainable ideal—perfect in all things—but as a much-needed model manifesting greatness of heart. This book is a celebration of the divine feminine as it manifests in a much-misunderstood form of spirituality. Denise Alvarado's love for Marie Laveau's work is evident. I am sure that Marie Laveau, the Mother of New Orleans Voodoo, returns the sentiment."
—Louis Martinié, author of *The New Orleans Voodoo Tarot and Waters of Return*

"New Orleans native Denise Alvarado brilliantly crafts a spiritually delicious reference book combining extensive historical research with a lifetime of personal experiences! Filled with snippets from the past, pearls of wisdom, and a detailed outline of Alvarado's "Laveau Voudou" tradition to which many readers will feel an immediate connection, *The Magic of Marie Laveau* is a valuable addition to any practitioner's bookshelf, especially those called to serve."

—Cairelle Crow, founder and coordinator of the
New Orleans Witches' Ball

"Whether you're a Marie Laveau devotee or are only beginning to learn about her, this is the book for you! Brimming with little known facts about her life, her relationships, and her charitable works, *The Magic of Marie Laveau* is much more than a well-researched biography. It also offers a plethora of valuable information for magical practitioners, including detailed instructions not only for working with her spirit, but also for performing many of the rituals and spells for which she is known. Reading this book truly changed my life—and I have no doubt that it will change yours as well."

—Dorothy Morrison, author of *Utterly Wicked*

PRAISE FOR *THE MAGIC OF MARIE LAVEAU*

"The Vodou community has been eagerly awaiting Denise Alvarado's fabulous addition to Marie Laveau's canon. Alvarado reaches deep into her academic, spiritual, and cultural backgrounds to provide us with a clear and resonant sense of the great Vodou Queen and her work. As an academic, she affords to Vodou the serious inquiry it deserves; as a practitioner, she gives a legitimate and informed insider's insight into traditions that merit respect. Because Alvarado knows her subject so well, she is able to bring Laveau to life for the reader. We feel a closeness to Marie Laveau, as if we walked and served with her in the New Orleans of the 1800s, and this also helps us to recognize her presence as she walks with us in our contemporary experience.

"Vodou is beautiful and life-affirming, and it is also practical. It has to help people endure life's challenges, just as it helped enslaved people endure the horrors of slavery. *The Magic of Marie Laveau* includes practical workings and "gris-gris" that provide a "hand up" to the reader in addition to lyrically presented and well-informed information about Laveau and the world in which she walked. I am grateful to Denise Alvarado for her years of research, her faithful devotion, and for her work to spread understanding and respect for Vodou and New Orleans' famous Queen, Marie Laveau. Respect and praise to Denise Alvarado!"

—Sallie Ann Glassman, author of *Vodou Visions* and cocreator and artist for *The New Orleans Voodoo Tarot*

"My bloodline has been in New Orleans—my hometown—for three hundred years and I proudly uphold the spirit of New Orleans Voodoo. I hail Mlle Marie and Le Grand Zombi every single day. Though my own Voodoo teachings vary from some presented in *The Magic of Marie Laveau*, I do not disagree with author Denise Alvarado's findings. As a priestess of New Orleans Voodoo and a full-time teacher of Marie, I can personally testify that it is near impossible to reconstruct her full magical life. It is no easy task to try to put oral traditions into words or to separate modern practices from those centuries old. It's even more difficult to sift the true Marie out from the sea of slander, secondhand information, and outside opinion that envelops her. Yet despite all of this, Denise has successfully combined both history and practical magic into one accessible book, making it possible for those far and wide to reach the Great Queen. *The Magic of Marie Laveau* brings Marie Laveau to life, adding further mystic lifeblood to her story. Long live Queen Marie Laveau!"

—Voodoo Queen Bloody Mary, author of *Bloody Mary's Guide to Hauntings, Horrors, and Dancing with the Dead* and curator of the New Orleans Haunted Museum

"*The Magic of Marie Laveau* is the ideal blend of the academic and the mystical. Denise Alvarado creates a historic understanding of how Mlle Laveau not only shaped the traditions and culture of New Orleans Voodoo but also influenced all Hoodoo and Conjure practices around the world. Through the biography of Mlle Laveau, Alvarado teaches that your daily spiritual practice and compassionate works are integral to your magical prowess. There is so much to learn in this book, reading it a second and third time is a must."

—Jacki Smith, author of *Coventry Magic with Candles, Oils, and Herbs,* and founder of Coventry Creations

"*The Magic of Marie Laveau* is a monumental piece of work. As an active member of the New Orleans Voodoo Spiritual Temple since 2000, I have venerated, served, and benefited from the spiritual force that is Marie Laveau in countless ways. I have striven to know and learn more about her throughout that entire time and continue to do so. *The Magic of Marie Laveau* is unique, as is the author Denise Alvarado, who, as an academic and a practitioner, marries both rivers into a wonderful book of impressive research, historical legacy, and hands-on magical work—something that is unprecedented in regard to Marie Laveau. I learned a great deal

To the Voodoo Queen of New Orleans,
Madame Marie Laveaux

Contents

Foreword

●●●

I am honored that Denise Alvarado invited me to write the foreword for *The Magic of Marie Laveau*. Denise is everything that I am not. Denise was born and raised in New Orleans with French, Spanish, and Native American family roots on the Gulf Coast of Mississippi and Costa Rica, with extensive experience in African and Native American religious and magical practices. I am not a native New Orleanian, not a person of color, and not an initiate or practitioner of the Afro-Creole religion of Voudou. I am, however, intensely interested in and respectful of the history of New Orleans' Creole families and the Voudou religion. Since 1995 I have spent much of my time in the church and civil archives of New Orleans, poring over handwritten eighteenth- and nineteenth-century French and Spanish documents or squinting at a microfilm reader while doing the research for my 2006 biography, *A New Orleans Voudou Priestess: The Legend and Reality of Marie Laveau* and my 2016 study, *Famille Vve Paris née Laveau: The Tomb of Marie Laveau in St. Louis Cemetery No. 1*.

Denise Alvarado's book *The Magic of Marie Laveau* is divided into three parts, the first of which is titled "La Belle de Nouvelle Orleans." An awful lot of hooey, ranging from factual errors to the most scurrilous sensationalism, was written about Marie Laveau in the past and is still being written today. Denise is not guilty of this sin. I wholeheartedly attest to the accuracy of her presentation of Laveau as a nineteenth-century New Orleans free woman of color—a daughter, wife, mother, grandmother, godmother, leader of the Voudou congregation, practicing Catholic, healer, philanthropist, businesswoman, and member of the Creole community.

There is only one subject on which Denise and I disagree: whether or not Marie Laveau was succeeded as the reigning Voudou Queen, known as "Marie II," by the younger of her two surviving daughters, Marie Philomène Glapion. I have argued against this theory, and Denise has argued in favor. In the end, the identity and even the existence of Marie II remains a mystery. Denise presents a good case, and I could be convinced.

"La Belle de Nouvelle Orleans" also describes "Laveau Voudou: A New Tradition," whereby Denise explains the emergence of Voudou in New Orleans, including the variations found among practitioners and specifically a style of Voudou she coins "Laveau Voudou." She interprets published sources from a practitioner perspective to identify spirits and characteristics associated with Marie Laveau and establishes a magicospiritual lineage for Laveau Voudou. This part sets the stage for the remainder of the book.

The second part instructs readers on "Becoming a Devotee" and "Developing a Respectful Servitude" of Marie Laveau. Honoring Marie does not require being a Catholic or a Voudou initiate. It does require recognizing her as an elevated Ancestor and adhering to her moral principles. I particularly applaud the "Walking the Path" section, which suggests ways of serving one's community as Marie would have done: by making rosaries; volunteering at a hospital, animal shelter, or veterans association; preparing bags of necessities for homeless people; and especially blessing dollar bills or coins and leaving them in strategic places to be found by those in need. This part also tells how to create an altar to Marie Laveau and how to offer prayers and petitions to her.

The third and longest part is "The Laveau Magicospiritual Legacy." Here I will entirely defer to Denise as an expert. Like me, she has drawn upon nineteenth-century newspaper articles and interviews conducted during the late 1930s and '40s by the Louisiana Writers' Project and the folklorist Harry Middleton Hyatt with elderly New Orleanians who knew Marie Laveau and her family. But to this "book knowledge" Denise also brings her own experience as an herbalist and a participant in African and Native American–based religions.

"The Laveau Magicospiritual Legacy" delineates twelve categories of conjure in the Laveau tradition that Denise has identified through careful examination of historical accounts, as well as current practices among practitioners. In doing so, Denise was able to establish an actual magico-spiritual legacy that links past practices to present tradition. This part tells how to assemble spells and charms in containers; perform candle magic; recite and adapt Christian (specifically Catholic) prayers in conjure work; use dolls; and work in the graveyard. More than simply a list of spells and formulas, this information is presented with a rationale for each category and historical evidence for its inclusion in Marie Laveau's spiritual legacy.

In *The Magic of Marie Laveau*, Denise Alvarado has separated the facts of Marie Laveau's life and legacy from the fantasies of some twentieth-century writers and persistent folk traditions that are sometimes not true. This is a goal we share in common. I hope readers will enjoy and benefit from their journey through the three parts of this valuable book—the history, the devotions, and the magick.

—Carolyn Morrow Long

Figure 1. Marie Laveau. *Collage by author*

Introduction

•••

If Marie Laveau[1] were alive today, I truly believe she would be at the forefront of the #MeToo and #BlackLivesMatter movements. I envision her standing in front of the White House as a #SisterResister, protesting the current administration's racist policies, and attacks on health care and the environment. Instead of Alyssa Milano, it could have been Marie Laveau sitting behind Brett Kavanaugh at those now infamous SCOTUS hearings that mobilized the female warrior aspect of the country like never before. She would be advocating prison reform, laying the gris gris down at the border for those seeking a better life or in need of asylum, and making sure no one forgets that there are children held in cages in internment camps for brown people right now, at this present moment, in post-slavery America.

But the reason she would be doing these things might surprise a lot of people who are unfamiliar with her as a living, breathing human being. Marie Laveau is no myth; she is no mere legend. While her reputation precedes her as the notorious Voudou[2] Queen of New Orleans, in reality, she was a free woman of color who ruled the city during antebellum New Orleans. This was no small feat. She was a devout Catholic, an independent businesswoman, a mother, and healer who lived her life in accordance with the corporal works of mercy. Stories abound about her magickal prowess, freeing men from the gallows and healing the sick from the brink of death. Her belief in Catholicism guided her life as well as her magick in such a distinct way that people from all over the world are inspired by her spirit and her story. This phenomenon is evidenced by the fact that her grave site is purportedly one of the most visited pilgrimage sites in the United States, second only to the King of Rock and Roll, Elvis Presley.

So, how does one begin to describe the legacy left by a legend? If the power of a person's life is in the stories they leave behind, then Marie Laveau has the market cornered as the most storied woman in the history of New Orleans.

First, the Voudou Queen's presence is obvious to anyone visiting the French Quarter in New Orleans. Shops are named for her, products are crafted bearing her name, ghost tours include her cottage and grave site, and practitioners take on her last name whether or not they possess any biological ties to her. Much to the chagrin of Christian adversaries, her name alone drives much of New Orleans' tourist industry. Her reputation for innovation and entrepreneurship, as well as her overall business acumen, served to fuel a niche market for herbalists, diviners, ritual performers, and Hoodoos that didn't exist before New Orleans was graced with her presence.

This hybrid commercial/spiritual space did not come without a price, however. The local police routinely harassed Laveau, but she kept them at bay with the mere threat of her conjure. And journalists often mocked the Voudous in local newspapers with the most salacious stories going viral the old-fashioned way, copied and redistributed in newspapers around the nation. Nonetheless, Marie Laveau excelled at navigating an oppressive, racist society. She walked gracefully as a Christian, just as easily as she danced with Li Grand Zombi, the sacred serpent.

Second, Marie Laveau is at the center of New Orleans' folklore. Her spirit can be seen in and around the city, flying over graves, dancing in cemeteries, walking down streets in the French Quarter, and haunting local shops. Take the story about Elmore Lee Banks, for example, who reportedly saw Marie Laveau's ghost one day in the mid-1930s near St. Louis Cemetery No. 1. As Banks recalled, an old woman dressed in a long white dress and wearing a blue tignon came into the drugstore where he was a customer and stood next to him. He had been telling the drugstore owner what he needed when he noticed the owner became bug-eyed and "ran like a fool into the back of the store." Not knowing what was going on, Elmore turned and looked at the old woman, who started laughing and laughing. Finally, the woman asked, "Don't you know me?" Elmore replied, "Why, no ma'am. Where did the drugstore man go?" Apparently, that was the wrong answer, because she suddenly slapped Banks upside the head. According to Banks, she then "jumped up in the air and went whizzing out the door and over the top of the telephone wires. She passed right over the graveyard wall and disappeared. Then I passed out cold." Banks said he was awakened to whiskey being poured down his throat by the proprietor, who told him, "That was Marie Laveau . . . she been dead for years and years but every now and then she come up in here where people can see her. Son, you just been slapped by the Queen of the Voodoos!" (Tallant 1946, 130–131).

Such is the stuff legends are made of, colorful oral history memorialized in the art and writings of pop culture. In fact, the term "Laveau legend" was used by Carolyn Morrow Long in her book *A New Orleans Voudou Priestess* in her deconstruction of the stories and myths that comprise the Marie Laveau historical narrative. It has also been used in common speech in New Orleans for as long as I can remember in reference to Marie Laveau's life and mythology. I use the term in this book in an effort to stay consistent with, and build upon, previous works.

Next, I make the case that Marie Laveau left a very specific legacy in her magick and spirituality. Yes, she has achieved rock star status in death, inasmuch as a Voudou Queen can achieve that status, but if we look at how she lived her life, she seemed to be more concerned with serving the people in her community than seeking recognition or fame. Evidence of her spiritual legacy can be seen in untold accounts written over the years of rootdoctors claiming to be descendants, relatives, or apprentices of Marie Laveau. They each profess unequivocally that the Hoodoo they do was the Voudou she did. Her legend is "kept alive by twentieth-century conjurers who claimed to use Laveau techniques, and it is kept alive through the continuing practice of commercialized voodoo in New Orleans" (Salzman, Smith, and West 1996, 3:1581). It is also kept alive through hybrid truth/fiction storylines found in books such as *The Voodoo Queen* and *Voodoo in New Orleans* by Robert Tallant. Writers and academics continue to rely on these storylines as primary sources of information. A participant in the Louisiana Writers' Project during the 1930s and '40s and one of Louisiana's best-known authors, Robert Tallant (1909–1957) had access to numerous interviews by people who knew Marie Laveau or were alive during her lifetime. Instead of adhering to facts in his books, he sensationalized much of the material and transformed it into popular novel format. His choice to do so influenced the Laveau legend perhaps more than any other single factor.

Tallant's writings, along with firsthand and secondhand accounts of Voudou ceremonies written by those who excelled in the kind of salacious writing characteristic of the *National Enquirer,* became part of the Laveau legend. Stories about wild sexual orgies and sacrificed black cats were recounted repeatedly in newspapers and books, while frenzied crowds of naked people were said to have fallen under Marie Laveau's evil Voudou spells. Marie and her Voudou religion were often demonized by an unforgiving press while others acknowledged her charity work and viewed her as a saint. When she attended a court hearing in 1873, for example, the newspaper described her as "dressed in all the soiled frippery of an impecunious princess" whose "eyes had all the seeming of a demon that was dreaming" (*The Daily State Journal* 1873).

Clearly, the propaganda of the 1800s fueled the public perception of Voudou, leaving us with a lack of factual information about Marie Laveau's life. One of her obituaries states, "The secrets of her life could only be obtained by the lady herself, but she would never tell the smallest part of what she knew" (*Boston Daily Globe* 1881). She did not write, so we have nothing of hers to read. What we have is oral tradition, old newspaper accounts, and interviews with elderly folks fifty-plus years away from her death. Moreover, she never had her photo taken despite rumors of an extant photo, so we have never seen what she truly looks like. On this issue her daughter, known as Madame Legendre[3], stated, "After her death an artist came and asked me to let him draw her . . . he wanted to copy some photograph . . . I told him she never had any taken nor ever been sketched" (*Times Picayune* 1886). As a result, a famous painting by Frank Schneider (a copy of the original by George Catlin long since lost) that hangs in the Cabildo in New Orleans became the most popular representation of Marie Laveau. But, those who actually saw her dispute this rendering. Alberta

Jefferson, one of Marie Laveau's childhood neighbors, described Marie as "a tall, thin, very pretty woman who wore her hair dressed with curls falling on her shoulder and never wore a headdress or tignon" (Breaux-McKinney 1937). Other descriptions of Marie range from the *New Orleans Republican's* "weird, mysterious looking being" to New Orleans' journalist George William Nott's "Voltairian look."

Today, there is the problematic tendency for scholars to rely on the reports and interpretations of outsiders to understand Marie Laveau and New Orleans Voudou, which leads to a seemingly endless cycle of myths and misunderstandings. Further, recent studies only focus on Voudou activity in the French Quarter and fail to understand that the city is not what defines New Orleans Voudou—it is the culture, practitioners, and Marie Laveau that do. In fact, New Orleans Voudou is more accurately called Creole Voudou as it extends far beyond the present-day boundaries of the city with several variations. These conditions place most of the current scholarly studies at least four degrees removed from the primary experience. To construct a more accurate understanding of what Voudou in New Orleans looked like in Marie Laveau's day, sources should include newspaper reports of a legal nature, such as court appearances and raids, and interviews conducted between 1936 and 1941 by the Louisiana Writers' Project with elderly folks who remembered her in the latter part of the nineteenth century. There are also a few informants interviewed by Harry Middleton Hyatt in his seminal work *Hoodoo-Conjuration-Witchcraft-Rootwork* that prove valuable, as does Zora Neale Hurston's work. All of the above and more are used in this book as foundation research to complement, but not replace, personal experience, understanding, and testimony of actual New Orleans Voudou practitioners.

In the past ten years, thanks to the impeccable research of Carolyn Morrow Long, Ina Fandrich, and others, we have more facts from which to build a more accurate picture of Marie Laveau's life. With each dot that is connected in her genealogy, and as more facts are substantiated, the more human she becomes. For devotees, the more elevated she becomes. As Zora Neale Hurston stated, "There is very little contemporary record of her, but her glory has not suffered with the passing of time" (Hurston 1931, 326). Her life has been explored, examined, and reimagined; and while the work on the level of the mundane moves forward, so does her spiritual devotion. As her energy is amplified and her spirit is elevated, her legacy is embraced globally as devotees set up shrines around the world, as far away as Australia, Canada, Great Britain, and the Netherlands.

There have been many books written about Marie Laveau that either focus on her life and legend or are popular spellbooks, pamphlets, or fictional novels. I wanted to write a different kind of book—one that describes Laveau's magickal and spiritual legacy with distinct practices found among her devotees, past and present. Hence, you will find in the following pages stylistic workings attributed to her as identified in the aforementioned sources along with oral tradition as a primary indigenous information source. In fact, the latter source of information—oral tradition by actual Voudou and Hoodoo practitioners—has been sorely lacking in the available literature.

What sets this book apart from others is that I am a born and bred New Orleans Creole, a cultural anthropologist as well as a life-long New Orleans Voudou insider with specialized knowledge of multiple folk traditions—a tradition keeper—which I have chosen to share with the world rather than take with me to my grave. My life experience precedes much of the current expression of Voudou in New Orleans proper. I learned on the bayous and in the city a secret religion that was not safe to share publicly during my youth. These facts allow me to bring to my readers a unique, twenty-first century, practitioner-scholar perspective that has been heretofore undocumented.

The mysteries of Marie Laveau's life and religion are encoded in her magick. Her legacy is embedded in the same rituals that have been passed down throughout the years since her death by practitioners of New Orleans Voudou. In this book, I decode some of these mysteries and make a case for a specific form of New Orleans Voudou called "Laveau Voudou" in a fresh presentation of her work. As such, the spiritual legacy of Marie Laveau is in the memory of her great name and in the inheritance of a powerful, unique magicospiritual tradition that largely defines Voudou in Louisiana today.

Part One

LA BELLE DE
NOUVELLE
ORLEANS

Figure 2. Marie Laveau as a young woman in the French Quarter. *Painting by author*

The Birth of a Queen

•••

Marie Laveau was a negress of café au lait tint, handsome in face, commanding in figure, and of remarkable intellect and force of character. She masqueraded as a hairdresser, thus learning the secrets of many a proud old New Orleans family. In helping sweethearts to secret meetings and forwarding clandestine correspondences, she had no equal and cared not whether the men and women she aided were old in coquetry and vice or young and innocent.

—*RICHMOND DAILY PALLADIUM, 1900*

I t is impossible to predict where our descendants will end up as a result of our life experiences. Marguerite, Marie Laveau's great-grandmother, was sold as a child from Senegal by African slave traders to Europeans and sent to the Americas in the belly of a slave ship. Who could have possibly known that as a result her great-granddaughter would become the leader of a new religion, elevate to the status of loa after death, and be revered globally?

Not much is known about Marguerite, but according to Carolyn Morrow Long, records indicate Marguerite and her daughter Catherine, age two, were listed in the property inventory of a white Creole named Henry Roche (aka Belaire) in 1756. Catherine's father is listed as a black man named Jean Belaire, about whom nothing further is known (Long 2016). He may have also been a slave of Henry Roche, as evidenced by the last name of Belaire. Slaves often took on the last name of their master because they were considered property and not recognized as having identities of their own.

Catherine, Marie's grandmother, grew up in Henry Roche's household and it is believed he fathered Catherine's mixed-raced children.

One of those children would become Marie's mother, named Marguerite, after her great-grandmother. Although I have never read it written this way, I think it is important to note that her children could likely be the product of rape, a common act of power and violence perpetrated by slave owners. Women were viewed as property, and sexual abuse and exploitation were rampant:

> Throughout the period of slavery in America, white society believed black women to be innately lustful beings. Because the ideal white woman was pure and, in the nineteenth century, modest to the degree of prudishness, the perception of the African woman as hypersexual made her both the object of white man's abhorrence and his fantasy. Within the bonds of slavery, masters often felt it their right to engage in sexual activity with black women. Sometimes, female slaves acquiesced to advances hoping that such relationships would increase the chances that they or their children would be liberated by the master. Most of the time, however, slave owners took slaves by force (Hallam 2004).

The nature of Catherine's pregnancy is further questioned by the fact that Catherine Henry "was at most thirteen years old when she gave birth to Marguerite, her first-born, who in turn was also at most thirteen when she had her first child. This calculation also indicates that Marguerite must have been born in the year 1783" (Fandrich 2005, 11). Coupling this probability with the fact that all of Catherine's children were born in bondage and she was sold and separated from them by unsympathetic owners further drives home the evidence of trauma. That Marie Laveau comes from this traumatic past with no one ever acknowledging it in such terms is tragic. She shares a common history of many African Americans in this country who descend from slaves. Let's call it what it is, acknowledge the intergenerational trauma she likely inherited, and pray for her mother, grandmother, and great-grandmother so that the Laveau family lineage may heal from their traumatic past. After all, so many people go to Marie for their own healing. How many do you think ever pray for hers?

Marie's grandmother Catherine is listed in the city records as a *marchande,* a purveyor of merchandise or foodstuffs that would have ranged from red brick dust to *calas* (a Creole fried rice pastry). After being sold by Henry Roche, Catherine ended up with two additional slave owners, until she ended up with a fourth in 1784, a free woman of color named Francoise Pomet. After eleven years with Pomet, Catherine was able to save up enough money to buy her freedom. In 1795, she paid $600 for her freedom and took Henry as her surname. She became a successful businesswoman in the marketplace, bought some land, and had the well-known house on St. Ann Street built between Rampart and Burgundy.

In 1790, Catherine's daughter, Marguerite Henry, was freed by her owner. She subsequently had several children with a Frenchman named Henri Darcantel, but he was not Marie's father. As a result of a brief relationship with a successful businessman named Charles Laveaux, Marie Catherine Laveaux was born on September 10, 1801. Marie's father, Charles Laveaux, though not acknowledged on her birth certificate as such, did acknowledge Marie as his daughter in numerous later documents (Fandrich 2005). Incidentally, Charles's mother was also named Marie Laveaux.

It is worth noting that the prevailing narrative in the Laveau legend describes Marie's father as a wealthy white planter, but this is not the case. He was a highly successful free man of color in the business of real estate and the slave trade. While Charles Laveaux's own father is not listed on his birth certificate either, it is likely he descended from Charles Trudeau dit Laveaux II (1743–1816), a white Creole who was the surveyor general of Spanish Louisiana from the early 1780s until he resigned in 1805.

Six days after her birth, Marie was baptized by Father Père Antoine into the Catholic faith at St. Louis Cathedral in New Orleans. Her grandmother Catherine took on the role of godmother to Marie. Her godfather was a Spanish man by the name of José Joaquin Velasquez, who was apparently the go-to guy when a slave or free person of color was in need of a godfather (Long 2006). Marie Laveau's baptismal certificate, which was written in longhand by Father Père Antoine, states:

> Maria, free mulatto—On this day, September 16, 1801, I, Fr. Antonio de Sedella, Capuchin Religious, Priest of the sanctuary of the Holy Church of the Cathedral of this city of New Orleans, baptize and give the holy oils to a girl child, free mulatto, who was born on the tenth of this month, daughter of Margarita, free mulatto, and an unknown father; I have exercised the sacred ceremony for this girl who received the name Maria; her godparents are José Joachim Velasquez and Catarina, free Negro, who will serve as her spiritual parents. Confirmed by Fr. Antonio de Sedella.

Credit for the discovery of Marie Laveau's birth and baptismal records goes to researcher Ina Fandrich, who, after fifteen years of searching, discovered them in the archives of the Archdiocese of New Orleans in 2001. Now that we have access to the documents, we can debunk two persistent myths that are part and parcel of the Laveau legend: 1) that she was nearly one hundred years old at the time of her death (she was seventy-nine); and 2) that she was born in Haiti (she was born in New Orleans). Nevertheless, in antebellum New Orleans the average life expectancy was twenty-something, and given Marie lived for nearly eighty years and spent her time helping people suffering from numerous plagues, it is understandable that she was assumed to have lived to the ripe old age of one hundred.

Unfortunately, there is scant information about Marie Laveau's childhood. She is believed to have grown up in Catherine's St. Ann Street cottage. On August 4, 1819, at the age of seventeen, she married a free man of color by the name of Jacques Paris, a carpenter by trade from San Domingue (a French colony in what is now present-day Haiti). According to the *Daily Picayune* obituary from June 17, 1881, Marie's marriage to Jacques Paris took place at the St. Louis Cathedral with Father Pére Antoine presiding and a lawyer by the name of Adolphe Mazureau reportedly standing in as witness. The obituary also states that she was twenty-five at the time of her wedding and that she was ninety-eight at the time of her death, which we now know is incorrect. Equally important, the attorney Mazureau did not start practicing law until 1830, nor was he "among the witnesses that are named in the actual marriage record in the St. Louis Cathedral archives" (Fandrich 2005, 304).

Mazureau did manage to find his way into the Laveau legend, however, as "a man of brilliant eloquence and dissolute habits . . . a favorite of hers, it being said by some that he was one of the most ardent of her youthful lovers (*Staunton Spectator and General Advertiser* 1881). Unconfirmed allegations such as these littered the local newspaper reports at the time, which punctuates the need for diligent fact-checking. These newspaper articles—in the absence of any other written documentation provided firsthand by family members or Marie—make up much of the available information about her life, and every researcher has incorporated them into their works, present company included.

According to local lore, Jacques and Marie were given a house on the 1900 block of North Rampart Street in the Faubourg Marigny by her father, Charles. And the famous gold hoop earrings that she wore were a gift from her father for her wedding. Though it was long assumed that Marie and Jacques did not have any children, there are two entries in the St. Louis Cathedral baptismal records that indicate otherwise. One daughter named Marie Angèlie Paris was born on November 27, 1822, a "free mulatto" and legitimate child of Jacques Paris and Marie Laveau. A second daughter named Felicité Paris was baptized on November 17, 1824. She was said to be seven years old, the daughter of the late Jacques Paris and Marie Lilavoix, an apparent spelling corruption of Laveaux (Long 2006). Felicité would have been born in 1817 when Marie was just sixteen years old, and two years prior to her marriage to Jacques Paris. What became of these two daughters is unknown; according to Carolyn Morrow Long, the St. Louis Cathedral funeral records for the years 1825 to 1829 have been lost.

Jacques Paris disappeared in 1824 and was presumed deceased, although documentation of his death or internment has never been located. The rumor mill suggests he went back to San Domingue, or that he signed a contract to be a merchant marine and was swept overboard. Others say he died in 1822 but wasn't in New Orleans at the time of his death

(Gandolfo 1992). Whatever the case may be, Marie became designated in official documents as La Veuve Paris, or the Widow Paris.

Following Jacque's disappearance, legend holds that Marie became a hairdresser, supporting herself by maintaining a clientele of wealthy white women. In this capacity, it is believed that she learned the secrets of local elites. Women would share their secrets with her, and Marie filed away the information for a rainy day. Though she was not listed in any public registry or census record as having practiced that profession, the belief holds true even today. Some of the major offerings given to Marie Laveau by modern devotees include combs, mirrors, makeup, and other items commonly associated with hairdressers.

About a year after Jacque's disappearance, Marie entered into a plaçage relationship with a wealthy white man named Louis Christophe Dominique Duminy de Glapion. Captain Glapion served with distinction during the war of 1815 as ordinance officer in the Battle of New Orleans under Andrew Jackson in the Ninth Native Regiment. Plaçage arrangements were commonplace among free women of color during her era due to Louisiana's anti-miscegenation law. Since interracial marriages were illegal, these types of arrangements allowed for white men to enter into long-term relationships with women of color, set up households, and provide for their care. While legend says they had fifteen children together, Marie and Christophe had just seven children from 1827 to 1838: Marie Eloise Euchariste, Marie Louise Caroline, Christophe, Jean Baptiste, Francois, Marie Philomene, and Archange. Only Eloise and Philomene survived to adulthood. Marie Philomene reportedly became her mother's successor in the world of New Orleans Voudou and is known as Marie Laveau II and Madame Legendre. Christophe died on June 26, 1855. It was said that after Christophe died, Marie turned to the Church more than ever before for consolation. Not only did she increase her own devotion, she brought others into its fold as well.

THE SLAVE OWNER

A little-known fact about Marie Laveau is that she and her domestic partner, Christophe Glapion, were slave owners. During the early antebellum period up until the Civil War, the illegal trafficking of slaves was rampant. The slave institution was undergoing changes that were influenced by a number of historical events, one of which was the Haitian revolution. As New Orleans was building its agriculture and business sectors with a proliferation of sugar and cotton plantations, there was a great demand for slave labor. However, the transatlantic slave trade ended in 1808, which ended the legal importation of enslaved people. Despite this new law, New Orleans remained a major site for human trafficking, which actually increased. Some of this activity involved the ongoing importation of enslaved human beings from the Caribbean, but Louisianans largely avoided importing slaves from Haiti specifically due to fear of their revolutionary spirit. They much preferred to receive enslaved people directly from Africa, as it was believed those human commodities wouldn't be under the influence of such radical ideas as overthrowing their white government. The slave market was further fueled from the resale of enslaved Africans from the upper south (North Carolina, Tennessee, Virginia, Kentucky, and West Virginia) to the lower Mississippi Valley, which extends from Cape Girardeau, Missouri, to the Gulf of Mexico.

Marie Laveau bore witness to an incredibly difficult time in history. Though she was born a free woman of color, her role as a slave owner meant she was subject to the restrictions of the Louisiana Black Code. Though we have no documented records of how she treated her slaves, my guess is that if she were a tyrant like the infamous Delphine LaLaurie, for example, it would have become part of the Laveau legend. Thus, the absence of horror stories in this regard seems to be a good thing.

The Louisiana Black Code or Code Noir was enacted in 1724 during the administration of Governor Bienville and was based on earlier codes developed in the French Caribbean colonies. The codes were designed to limit the freedom of African Americans in the colony, to prevent desertion, and ensure the availability of a cheap labor force following the abolishment of slavery during the Civil War. Slave owners were mandated to baptize their slaves in the Catholic faith and to give them Sundays off for worship. Slaves were allowed to marry, separation of families was not permitted, and slave owners were not allowed to severely beat or murder the enslaved. While the French laws provided greater rights to slaves than their British and Dutch counterparts, Louisiana's law differed in several negative ways. They restricted the movement of people of African descent and stipulated that the status of people with darker skin was always lower than those with lighter complexions. Additionally, it intentionally thwarted contact between racial groups. There were also articles within the Code Noir that were intended to ensure the safety and wellbeing of slaves as merchandise so that they could be productive workers. While the Code Noir allowed slaves to report to authorities if they were not given these basic provisions, reports were rare and instead the enslaved often resorted to running away. The runaway slaves were referred to as Maroons.

In 1811, Marie Laveau was about ten years old and Louisiana was still the Territory of Orleans. The largest slave revolt in American history, referred to as the German Coast Uprising, occurred about thirty miles outside of the city that year. Enslaved men rebelled against the harsh conditions of the sugar plantations, even though they should have been protected by the Louisiana Black Code. Between two hundred and five hundred enslaved men armed with mostly hand tools participated in the march from the sugar plantations on the German Coast toward New Orleans (Genovese 1976). Along the way, they burned five plantation houses, several sugar houses, and crops. The rebels ended up only killing two white men. Confrontations with white militias and soldiers hunting down the slaves, however, ended in the execution and decapitation of more than one hundred of the rebels, whose heads they publicly displayed in an effort to intimidate and discourage further revolts (Rasmussen 2011).

While President Abraham Lincoln's Emancipation Proclamation had theoretically abolished slavery in 1863, it was officially abolished by the state constitution of 1864, during the American Civil War. Marie Laveau was born a free woman of color, but for most of her life slavery was alive and well. It was commonplace for free people of color to own slaves, and almost all New Orleanians of means did so. Some bought slaves and allowed them to work for hire elsewhere while collecting a percentage of their wages, while others were purchased as household servants.

The issue of motivation behind Marie Laveau's status as a slave owner is unknown. It is highly likely that experiencing the events of her childhood as a possible witness to the uprising impacted her into adulthood. Just as those of us who lived during the attacks of September 11 will always be affected by them, whether we lived in New York City or on the Gulf Coast, Marie had to have been affected by the largest slave revolt in American history. There is no evidence Marie was involved in the slave trade prior to her partnership with Christophe Glapion, but there is archival evidence that he was involved in the buying and selling of slaves prior to being with Marie (Long 2006). This is not surprising, as he was French, and the French embraced slave ownership as part of their culture. Since 1706, chattel slavery had been perpetrated against Native populations in Louisiana until 1768 when, under Spanish rule, the enslavement of indigenous peoples was banned. This ban did not include Africans or people of African descent, however. Spanish rule did eventually introduce *coartación*, a new law that allowed slaves to buy their freedom and freedom for other slaves. It was under this law that Marie's grandmother Catherine was able to purchase her freedom in 1795.

Once Marie and Christophe became a couple, they bought and sold eight slaves (Long 2006). Like most other slave owners of their time, they bought slaves, kept them for a little while, and then sold them, often at a profit. There are no reports or articles available to tell us how they treated their slaves. However, the idea has been put forth that the Laveau-Glapion home served as a Southern depot for the Underground Railroad and that they helped to free slaves. Marie is known through oral history to have provided slaves with charms to protect them on their journeys to freedom.

Marie and Christophe continued buying and selling slaves until 1854, when Christophe sold his final enslaved woman. If Marie was involved in assisting slaves in their quest for freedom, it would make sense that she would not compel Christophe to stop buying and selling slaves—that would be a red flag to outsiders, as it was something he was known for doing prior to being with her. Why she participated during their time together is a more difficult question to answer. Although it could be that finances would not permit it, it is noteworthy that Marie did not participate in the slave trade after Christophe's final sale in 1854, or after his death in 1855.

Voudou is a signifying science—signs, symbols, codes, and signifiers are embedded in the tradition. Support for Marie Laveau as an abolitionist or even a station master for the Underground Railroad and the Laveau-Glapion home as a safe house comes from one very small, yet significant clue recalled by a man named Charles Raphael, born in 1868. He describes the altar in her front room, which had items on it like "good luck charms, money-making charms, and husband-holding charms." He adds, "On this altar she had a statue of St. Peter and St. Marron, a colored saint." All safe houses in the Underground Railroad network held signifiers to indicate it was a safe space for fugitive slaves such as passwords, call-and-response songs, coded knocks on doors, and quilts bearing special designs. These types of signals would have been easy to mask the already foreign Voudou activity going on at the home. But it is the presence of a statue of St. Maroon that screams the loudest, because St. Maroon is the patron saint of runaway slaves.

To put it into a modern context, if we look at how various Latin American folk saints are found among drug dealers and smugglers today, we can see some parallels. For example, some drug dealers and users alike believe that having a statue of Jesús Malverde nearby renders their drug stash invisible. Law enforcement agrees that a "Malverde statue in the home of an already suspected drug dealer is considered a red flag to officers, indicating illegal substances may be on the premises" (Davis 2007). Likewise, the presence of a statue of St. Maroon in the home would signify someone sympathetic to the abolitionist movement.

In New Orleans Voudou and folk Catholicism, it is common practice to pair up saints according to purpose. For example, St. Expedite, the patron saint of expediency, may be paired with St. Jude, the patron saint of hopeless causes, to ensure petitions to St. Jude are answered with haste. St. Expedite is "sent in" with St. Jude to make the case with Bon Dieu (God) on behalf of the petitioner. This ritual dynamic is tantamount to a spiritual buddy system whereby the saints benefit from each others' special talents while the petitioner benefits from their combined efforts. Petitioning St. Jude alone does not guarantee expediency; in fact, he can be slow to work at times. So, if a petitioner needs a seemingly hopeless case addressed quickly, St. Expedite can make it happen. Now, if we consider the two saints on Marie Laveau's altar in the context of Voudou and folk Catholicism, we can parse out what is going on as it relates to assisting runaway slaves. First, we have St. Peter, who is syncretized with Papa Legba. St. Peter holds the keys to the kingdom of heaven, while Papa Legba holds the keys to the spirit world. These two energies are tapped into in Voudou when there are obstacles that are in need of removal, roads that need to be open, and secrets that need to be kept under lock and key. The keys also signify the ability to unlock the chains of slavery. Thus, St. Peter holds the keys to what fugitives referred to as "heaven" (which referred to freedom in Canada), and St. Maroon provides protection on the freedom train.

THE HAIRDRESSER

Wherever there was a skeleton in the family closet Marie held the key. But she was true to the confidence reposed in her and did not turn her knowledge to any unjust advantage. She knew of many proud homes where a whisper concerning the taint of colored blood would have spread consternation, but she was silent and did not even extort money for not overthrowing their standing in society.

—STAUNTON SPECTATOR AND GENERAL ADVERTISER, JUNE 21, 1881

According to the Laveau legend, Marie became a hairdresser after the assumed death of her husband, Jacques Paris. Carolyn Morrow Long (2006) reports that there are no records on file confirming this rumor to be true; however, it was a common occupation among Creole women at the time, so it is not a far-fetched assumption. There were also people interviewed from the Louisiana Writers' Project who remembered her in that capacity. For example,

Theresa Kavanaugh, born around 1860, said, "Marie Laveau called herself a hairdresser, and that's how she got in the good graces of fine people." Another woman, Mary Washington, born in 1863, remembered Marie as "some kind of hairdresser and seamster, but she did all that in her early days. . . . Her associating with white people made her know how to fool them."

As a hairdresser, Marie had the opportunity to network among the city's bourgeoisie as she was invited into their homes to fix their hair. She reportedly paid off poor black servants, effectively turning them into moles, in exchange for inside information. The information she gleaned from the impromptu confessions of wealthy white women gave her an edge in her Voudou and conjure work. Using these types of natural and manufactured methods of gathering intel, she gained inside knowledge of who was who in the upper echelons of society—who cheated on who, who was whose real baby daddy, and who was interracial but *passé blanc*. She held the secrets close in heart and mind; no doubt filed away for a rainy day when someone approached her for help in the future. Even so, the community perception was such that no matter how big or potentially scurrilous the secret, they knew she held the keys to the closets that held everyone's scandalous skeletons. And that type of public perception is powerful, whether or not it is true, as the *Staunton Spectator and General Advertiser* reported on June 21, 1881:

> Coming in daily contact with the best-informed men of that period, and possessing a remarkably retentive memory, it is no wonder that she acquired a large store of valuable information. She was by no means backward in delivering her opinions, and as her predictions nearly always came true, and the course she suggested generally proved the wisest, Marie soon possessed a larger clientele than the most astute and far-seeing legal counselor.

As with all things Laveau, there are a number of superstitions associated with the activities of hairdressers. For example, it is dangerous to throw hair-combings away instead of burn them—because birds may weave them into their nests, and while the nest remains the person to whom the hair belonged will have a continual headache (Hearn 1886). Since throwing hair away is not an option, it was customary to burn a client's hair after cutting it instead. A Voudouist could read how the hair burned and relate it to the person's course in life. When hair lights up and burns in a blaze of glory, it signifies a long, happy life. But if the hair fails to catch fire or burns really slow and low, it means significant illness and death are inevitable.

Marie Laveau's ability to maneuver in society in ways that were advantageous to her livelihood was impressive, but there are those who derided her for those activities, placing her in the category of con woman as opposed to cunning woman. However, this is a matter of perception. Marie Laveau gathered information about her demographic by building alliances and networking like any smart businessperson does. She marketed her talents through word of mouth and showed up in places where she would be remembered, such as sickrooms, courthouses, and the marketplace. She built her clientele across racial lines and invited white people into her fold. Most importantly, she had satisfied customers and got great results. All of the things she reportedly engaged in during her time were necessary for success in business. If her activities were put in these terms instead of tabloid fashion, her authenticity as a Voodoo Queen would never be questioned (Alvarado 2011, 51).

THE LAVEAU COTTAGE

She lives in a quiet little alley running out from Marais street, overhung by old tumble-down buildings, redolent with evidences of decay. The green moss of nearly half a century covers the roofs and the casing, the windows and the door-steps reek with accumulated damps. Now and then on sunshiny days a few straggling rays of light penetrate the gloomy alley with ineffectual attempts to make visible the surroundings. But dusk and gloom are the prevailing characteristics of the place.

—NEW ORLEANS REPUBLICAN, 1873

Marie Laveau's childhood home at 152 St. Ann Street remained her primary residence until her death in 1881. In fact, the cottage housed the Laveau family for nearly one hundred years (1798–1897). Her grandmother, Marguerite Henry, purchased the lot in 1798 and had the house built with the money she earned as a marchande. The cottage was set back from the street and surrounded by a tall wooden fence with an ample yard on the left and in the back. It was a "square, one-story structure with four out-buildings, one of which is one and a half stories" (Long 2011, 67). Thus, she had plenty of space to help those in need of a place to crash, either temporarily or longer term. According to several interviews conducted by the Louisiana Writers' Project, Marie allowed many of the Choctaw merchant women to camp out in her backyard in one of the outbuildings and provided shelter for slaves in need of a safe place.

The facts show that Marie's grandmother had the house on St. Ann Street built as a result of her blood, sweat, and tears. Upon her death, however, the house went into probate and a creditor came forward claiming the estate had owed him due to a lingering debt. Upon Catherine Henry's passing and her debt coming to light, her son, grandson, and Marie Laveau decided to put the house up for auction to pay off Catherine's creditor. It was purchased by Christophe Glapion, who allowed Marie's family to continue living there.

Though the original structure is no longer standing, the site of Marie Laveau's home on St. Ann Street is important in understanding how and where she grew up. Moreover, descriptions of her home give us some clues as to her conjure and Voudou practice. And as may be expected, the site is laden with legend that is infinitely more exciting than reality.

For example, an enduring part of the Laveau legend related to her home can be attributed to George William Nott (1869–1946), who promoted a magickal version of how the house came to be inhabited by the Voodoo Queen. As the story goes, it all started when a young man from an afflu-ent family was in some real legal trouble. The evidence against him was very strong, so his father went to Marie Laveau for help. He promised to reward her handsomely if she would get his son out of trouble. On his son's court date,

The sorceress entered the St. Louis Cathedral at dawn and knelt at the altar rail for several hours, three Guinea peppers in her mouth. Then, she crept into the Cabildo next door and deposited the peppers under the judge's chair. The youth was dismissed, and the happy father presented Marie with a small cottage on St. Ann Street between North Rampart and Burgundy Streets, almost adjacent to Congo Square. There, Marie Laveau was to live until her death (Tallant 1946, 58).

In 1873, eight years before her death, a description of the inside of Marie Laveau's home was printed in the *New Orleans Republican*. The description matches what has been passed down in oral tradition about the location of working altars where workers customarily have a private area for conjuring, out of the sights of others. Whispers of rooms hidden behind beaded curtains or in the back rooms of laundromats in New Orleans, for example, correspond to the types of configurations found in the homes of professional conjure workers and Spiritualists.

It is not uncommon among workers to have a decidedly more Catholic-appearing altar in the front of the house and a working conjure altar in a back room. Working altars are often not very pretty and may contain unsightly items like animal parts and jars of unsavory potions. Further, it is standard practice to keep spellwork out of sight lest foreign energies dilute, pollute, or otherwise interfere with the power of the working. To those unfamiliar with the inner workings of the Voudou Queen and conjure work, the imagination runs wild, fueling the legend:

The first glance into this desolate-looking, out-of-the way abode would chill the beholder with a sort of superstitious awe. The supernatural seems to have stamped it with an indelible impression. . . . The room is scantily furnished. A few chairs, an old table, a jug of water, and some coarse prints are all. A chintz curtain hides a doorway leading into an adjoining room; but into this apartment no visitor has ever entered. It is sacred to incantation, and, as the superstitious believe, to the association of evil spirits (*New Orleans Republican* 1873).

The house at 1020 St. Ann Street only marks the approximate site of the original home, then numbered 152 Rue St. Ann (as shown by Marie Laveau's death certificate). While the original Laveau cottage was torn down in 1903, a new structure was built on the same foundation as the original (Gandolfo 1992). In the paranormal world, it is believed that residual energy from Marie Laveau and those who resided with her are still connected to that location. The home is featured on haunted tours of New Orleans, where tour guides share stories of Marie Laveau's ghost walking down St. Ann Street, wearing a long white dress and her signature white tignon, tied in seven points to signify a crown.

THE DEVOUT CATHOLIC

Marie had a large, warm heart and tender nature, and never refused a summons from the suffering, no matter how dangerous the disease. Wherever she went, she labored faithfully and earned life-long friends. During the yellow fever and cholera epidemics she proved herself a noble woman, going from patient to patient, administering to the wants of each and saving many from death.

—STAUNTON SPECTATOR AND GENERAL ADVERTISER, JUNE 21, 1881

Marie Laveau's life and works embody what the Catholic Church calls corporal works of mercy—charitable actions that help our neighbors in their bodily needs, such as feeding the hungry, giving drink to the thirsty, clothing the naked, sheltering the homeless, visiting the sick, visiting the imprisoned, and burying the dead. These principles of right living are derived from the teachings of Jesus and are altruistic actions we are to engage in to treat other people as if they are Christ in disguise. Marie Laveau lived in accordance with the works of mercy in how she lived her life in service to her community. As we examine Marie Laveau's life, we can see how she engaged in these core principles in her life's work.

Figure 3. Father Père Antoine. *Credit: Image first appeared in Henry C. Castellanos,* New Orleans As It Was: Episodes of Louisiana Life *(New Orleans: The L. Graham Limited Co., Ltd., Publishers, 1905)*

For example, Marie is on record for nursing yellow fever and cholera patients during the city's epidemics, and she provided housing and food for the poor. She sponsored education for children and even adopted one little boy and posted bond for free women of color accused of petty crimes. She visited condemned prisoners, set up altars on the inside, and prayed with them during their final hours. We now know she also offered the use of her tomb to strangers who had no burial place of their own. In fact, her tomb in St. Louis Cemetery No. 1 where she is buried is the resting place for a grand total of eighty-four people! Only twenty-five of those buried there are verified or assumed to be family members (Long 2016).

The charitable deeds of Marie Laveau are etched in the memory of the city alongside the Catholic priest Father Père Antoine. Together, they are known for ministering to the sick and incarcerated. In addition to his work with the infirm, Père Antoine shared Marie Laveau's dedication to the poor, imprisoned, and enslaved. Their relationship began when Marie Laveau was just a baby and he baptized her. He was obviously an important figure in her life, as he also married her to Jacques Paris. Given their shared activities of service to the community, it is likely he schooled Marie in the principles of the Catholic faith. They had a close relationship and even worked out a deal where she could do some ritual work behind the church every Sunday:

> After masses on Sunday, Marie performed light rituals in St. Anthony's garden behind the St. Louis Cathedral. She promised her followers these rituals as a reward for coming to Church with her. Father Pére Antoine approved of what Marie was doing because she would encourage Voodoos to come back to mass, unlike the other Voodoo leaders who discouraged their followers from going to Church (Gandolfo 1992, 18).

Père Antoine was in service of St. Louis Cathedral for more than forty years as a Capuchin priest from 1785 to 1790 and again from 1795 until his death.

Marie Laveau is often described as being a devout Catholic or having returned to Catholicism and abandoned Voudouism in her elderly years. In some ways, this trend appears to project a discomfort in fully acknowledging Voudou as a legitimate religion by using Catholicism as the legitimizing platform for comparison. It's as if to say it is okay she was a Voudou because she was also a devout Catholic. The emphasis in syncretism follows where we all acknowledge her devotion to St. Peter and Mother Mary and attribute her altruism to her Catholic faith and works of mercy instead of considering the nature of Voudou and its inherent precepts of healing and curing. I would like to propose an alternate view as food for thought.

Marie Laveau likely had Voudou in some form in her lineage. Her great-grandmother Marguerite is believed to have come from Senegal and may have passed on some of her herbal and talismanic knowledge to her daughter Catherine, who in turn passed on her gifts to Marie's mother Marguerite, who in turn passed them on to Marie. The passing on of indigenous knowledge in this fashion is a natural and expected process. In addition, there are reports of Marie Laveau as a student and business associate of Doctor John Montenee, who was the reigning gris gris man in her time. As a result, she would have been well schooled in the art of conjure and local Voudou culture. As she was born in a time when Catholicism was the mandated religion, she had no choice but to learn the tenets of the faith, and so she would have been instructed by the Ursuline nuns and Father Pére Antoine.

But Marie was no stranger to the cloaking secrets of Voudouism in New Orleans at the time. It is not surprising at all to see St. Peter exemplified in reports of her Voudou ceremonies, as he is associated with Papa Legba, a primary Voudou loa and African god essential to the practice of Voudou on any level. To invoke the spirits, one must always invoke Papa Legba first because he, like St. Peter, holds the keys to the spirit world. Today, we call him Papa Legba; but in Marie's time, he was called Papa Labas, Labat, or Limba. The name Limba is rarely used now as far as I know; however, Labas can be heard during Mardi Gras season with exuberant shouts along the parade routes: "Eh, Labas!" A traditional New Orleans song sung originally in Creole, it has a call-and-response style with the words translated as "Hey, over there!" I posit it is a reference to St. Peter and Papa Legba. Most people have no idea that they are shouting out to Papa Legba, the opener of roads in New Orleans Voudou, because the words have been translated and interpreted by non-practitioners of Voudou who are unaware of the contextual root of the words.

The extent to which Marie Laveau used her Catholic faith to make her Voudou practice more palatable to Christians in mainstream society is impossible to know. However, it is deserving of the same consideration as the emphasis on her role as a devout Catholic.

NURSING THE SAFFRON SCOURGE

She was very successful as a nurse; wonderful stories being told of her exploits at the sick bed. In yellow fever and cholera epidemics she was always called

upon to nurse the sick, and always responded promptly. Her skill and knowledge
earned her the friendship and approbation, of those sufficiently cultivated, but the
ignorant attributed her success to unnatural means and held her in constant dread.

—Daily Picayune, June 18, 1881

Sixty-seven yellow summers thrived in New Orleans between the years 1796 and 1905. This was the period of time that yellow fever, also known as the Saffron Scourge, Yellow Jack, Black Vomit, and the strangely descriptive Bronze John on his Saffron Steed, plagued the city and haunted its citizens. At the time no one knew how the disease spread, and many fled the city for the Mississippi Gulf Coast or Grande Isle. Others who succumbed to the illness were burned or buried. Fifty thousand people reportedly died, and their bodies were stacked one upon another in the cemeteries. The stench of death permeated the streets. At one point, people were dying faster than graves could be dug, giving rise to the popular saying, "Pretty soon people would be digging their own graves." Even without the deaths caused by disease, however, the streets of New Orleans were frequently reported to be unsanitary and littered with trash, dead animals, rats, and cockroaches. Raw sewerage was dumped into the Mississippi River, which was the city's source of drinking water. It's not hard to imagine how a plethora of illnesses and diseases spread, given the utter lack of sanitary conditions.

Indeed, New Orleans saw more than her share of diseases. In addition to yellow fever, other diseases such as cholera, smallpox, bronchitis, Bright's disease, typhus, dysentery, and tuberculosis were present. The city's close proximity to bayous, swamps, and lakes made it ripe for mosquito infestations. One of the confounding things about the Saffron Scourge, though, was that it did not kill everyone. It seemed that many of the locals developed a resistance and were largely unaffected by it—or at least, they did not die from it. Thus, the disease became known as the Stranger's Disease. Treatments for the illness included wearing camphor around the neck, carrying garlic, doing full-body soaks in vinegar, chewing quinquinia, and burning tar at night to "purify the air." Physicians' treatments at the time tended to hasten death rather than prevent it. Their treatments consisted of bloodletting, leeching, purging, and mercury consumption, which had disastrous consequences. Sadly, mercury treatments caused the fatalities of multitudes of military men in 1812. There were so many deaths that the St. Anthony of Padua Chapel, known today as Our Lady of Guadalupe, was built in front of the St. Louis Cemeteries in 1826 specifically to handle funerals. The church soon earned another name: the Mortuary Chapel.

Marie Laveau is well known for her compassionate care for nursing the sick during these public health crises. Her healing methods would have likely consisted of the folk variety—energy-giving methods, as opposed to the energy-draining methods of the physicians. Herbal teas, blancmange, and nourishing soups, along with baths, massage, and prayer, were the mainstay of Afro-Creole nurses at the time. One remedy used the main herb for the Hoodoo formula Louisiana Van Van—vervain, or verbena. This herb was grown for medicinal purposes and folk magic uses in the courtyard of the New Orleans Pharmacy:

> A remedy for yellow fever has been discovered at Angostura, Venezuela. The remedy is the plant vervain or verbena, which grows abundantly in that region. The expressed juice of the leaves given in small doses three times a day, with an enema of the same every two hours, is stated to be a perfect cure for the yellow fever and black vomit, even in their most threatening stages. All the physicians of Angostura have adopted this treatment of the disease, and they state that hardly any deaths occur under its influence . . . ("Remedy for Yellow Fever" 1853).

Marie Laveau's skill as a healer in herbal medicine was renowned. When cholera wreaked havoc in New Orleans, she was credited with saving hundreds of lives. The cramps associated with cholera had to be broken within ten minutes or the afflicted would die, and her remedy reportedly did the trick. She is said to have "made a 'charm' of brimstone, tar, and feathers, and lighted it under the noses of those persons who were sick, and it would 'immediately and perceptibly abate the cramp'" (Dillard Project 1942, 46). But she was not alone in this knowledge. Many Creole women had exceptional curative abilities. In fact, the success rate of these women was nothing short of magickal for those suffering from any number of the horrible illnesses prevalent at the time. White doctors and outsiders in general were both curious and envious of their knowledge and the power their skill afforded them:

> Their herb-decoctions, tisanes, vegetable teas, vegetable sudorifics and aperients, vegetable nerve medicines and vegetable cures for skin diseases are simply wonderful. The skill of the Creole women in natural medicine is extraordinary and of the highest importance. I tried to induce one to give me a recipe. She refused. It was her secret, she said, which she would impart only to her children. Is it wonderful that many of these excellent nurses are suspected of being able to use their knowledge for deadly and secret purposes? (Buel 1883, 535)

The above quote illustrates both the desire to appropriate indigenous knowledge as well as the tendency to cast a shadow over the Creole nurses' skill as healer. Characterizing their work as "deadly and secretive" reflects the dichotomous nature of the Catholic faith: good versus evil and God versus Satan. Those who were invested in demonizing Marie Laveau attributed her success to unnatural means, held her in constant dread, and highlighted the strange remedies practiced by conjure women. And although Voudou was tolerated by the church on the surface, there was a clear goal to ultimately shut it down in its entirety:

> The great and festering sore of voodooism afflicting the negroes calls for all our zeal, as Catholics, to help the bishops and clergy in the South, and the English society that has entered this field; by prayer, by material aid, by earnest and sustained efforts to preserve the purity of faith among colored Catholics ("St. Francis of Assisi" 1877, 11).

Protestants in the South espoused similar rhetoric when it came to Voudou. According to one Protestant Episcopal bishop from Kentucky, "Their religion is a superstition, their sacraments are fetishes, their worship a wild frenzy, and their morality a shame" (Oliver 1885, 87). Today, the Catholic and Protestant churches are slightly more flexible with regards to accepting traditional African and indigenous religions, whereas the Pentecostals are not. Pentecostals call for a complete rebuke of traditional religion and spirituality and demand the complete embrace of a colonial Christian God.

Some of the remedies used by Creole women in nursing common maladies such as colds, fever, flu, and headaches were informed by years of practicing folk medicine. Many of the formulas were learned from local Native Americans and others were adapted to the new environment by Africans. A common fallacy is that Africans were unfamiliar with the local flora and fauna and had to learn everything from scratch. This is not true. They brought much knowledge with them, as well as the seeds for certain plants. Creole remedies represent the best of a healing collaboration between Africans, Native Americans, and local Cajun *traiteurs* (treaters). Many of the remedies relied on the healing properties of a single herbal ingredient while others were multibotanical compounds. In addition, Louisiana Creole folk healing exists on a continuum of herbal curatives to healing through prayer. Most of the time, remedies consisted of a combination of the two.

PRISON MINISTRY AND COURT WORK

She was often placed on the stand to testify concerning such matters, but no threats of imprisonment could force her to unseal her lips. It was only where the families had become haughty and arrogant, and were cruel and brutal to their dependents, that she told all she knew, and her disclosures brought terrible disgrace upon those who had called forth her wrath.

—Staunton Spectator and General Advertiser, June 21, 1881

The Marie Laveau legend is replete with stories about her knack for winning court cases with her gris gris. I shared one popular story about how she was given her home on St. Ann Street in the previous section The Laveau Cottage. As with many tall tales, there are as many versions of the story as there are people telling it. According to another version of the story, Marie was approached by a man one day in 1830 after being referred to her by his attorney. The man was desperate. His son had been charged with the rape of a young woman, and the sentence for rape at the time was death by hanging. The young woman came from an affluent family, and the man's family was neither wealthy nor influential. He told Marie that both he and his son believed the boy would lose and surely be convicted. Having very little hope that they could overcome the issue without Marie's help, the boy's father promised to give Marie his house on St. Ann Street and as much money as he could gather. Of course, Marie was a savvy businesswoman, so she wouldn't simply agree to those terms without getting all the facts of the case. She told the boy's father that she would get back to him after she had a chance to speak to the boy and his attorney. After consulting with the two men, she concluded that it was the girl's father who had charged the boy with rape, not the girl. So, believing the young man was innocent, she agreed to take the case and accepted the father's offer.

It is said she made three gris gris bags and strategically placed them in the courtroom before the trial. As with all the cases she took, Marie won. The young man was found innocent, and she was given the house on St. Ann Street.

We now know that this story is not true, because that house on St. Ann Street was actually purchased by Marie's mother, Catherine, and was Marie's childhood home. Still, it makes for a great little story that showcases the legendary power of Marie Laveau's court case gris gris.

It was during her early years with Christophe Glapion, though, that Marie began to gain a good reputation for her gris gris with regards to court cases. It seemed she always had favorable outcomes in cases in which she worked her mojo, and the locals took notice. When she took on a client, she won. Her winning was attributed to her skill in the art of magick, as well as having inside knowledge of the private lives of the local judges and others in positions of power.

In fact, when she wasn't nursing the sick during one of the many outbreaks of disease plaguing the city, Marie Laveau made it a priority to visit prisoners on death row and provide spiritual guidance:

Marie would often visit the cells of the condemned and turn the thoughts of those soon to be led out to atone for their crimes to their Saviour. Her coming was considered a blessing by the prisoners, because if they could only excite her pity, her powerful influence would often obtain their pardon, or at least a commutation of sentence (*Staunton Spectator and General Advertiser* 1881).

The Parish Prison was a slave institution. There, the unforgiven awaited their impending executions in sadness, resignation, darkness, and despair. But walking onto death row, where only the worst of criminals resided, was a normal part of Marie Laveau's service to her community. In May 1871, for example, she became involved in the death row cases of Pedro Abriel and Vincent Bayume. She arrived at the formidable prison with white cloth, flowers, candles, and decorations in hand. For three days, she constructed powerful altars of penance for the men, decorating them in a manner that endures as a traditional altar style in New Orleans Voudou. The three-tiered altars she constructed are described in an article published in the *New Orleans Daily Picayune*:

For more than twenty years, whenever a human being has suffered the final penalty in the Parish Prison, an old colored woman has come to their cell and prepared an altar for them. This woman is Marie Laveau, better known as a Priestess of the Voudous. Arriving at the prison yesterday morning, she proceeded at once to prepare an altar for the worship of the men who have been sentenced to expiate the guilt of murder on the scaffold. It consists of a box of about three feet square; above this are three pyramidal boxes, rising to a small apex on which is placed a small figure of the Virgin.

The entire altar is draped in white; on each end of the shelving is a vase of green and white artificial flowers, and beside these a smaller vase of pink and white camelias. In the center rests a prayerbook in Spanish, and framed in gold, leaning against the altar are hung saints' pictures around the walls of the cell. Before the altar is drawn a curtain of white muslin, deeply fringed in silver filigree. The aspect of the altar is singularly beautiful and simple. (*New Orleans Daily Picayune* 1871).

This article gives us one of the only direct references to how Voudou altars were constructed at the time of Marie Laveau. Fast-forward to modern-day New Orleans, and we can observe altars continuing to be constructed in the three-tiered fashion, with flowers, the Virgin Mary, and other Catholic icons and paraphernalia present. The Spanish prayer book that is referenced was most likely a Catholic missal or a Spiritualist prayer book as both religions were present in New Orleans at the time. Prayer books are still kept on altars, with the Bible and Spiritualist librettos being popular among practitioners.

MARIE LAVEAU II

The Laveau legend has caused much confusion about mother and daughter, resulting in a conflation of the two women. The general public, as well as present-day devotees who are unfamiliar with her history, often confuse Marie Catherine Laveau with her daughter, Marie Philomene Glapion (Madame Legendre), commonly referred to as Marie Laveau I and II, respectively. Popular lore says Marie Laveau held the magickal powers of eternal youth. This myth stems from her daughter, Marie Philomene, the spitting image of her mother, reportedly stepping in and carrying on as Voudou Queen Marie II.

Like pretty much everything to do with the Laveau legend, there is some discrepancy about the identity of the second Voudou Queen Marie Laveau. Marie Laveau had two daughters with Christophe Glapion with the name Marie: Marie Heloïse (born 1827, died 1862) and Marie Philomene (born 1836, died 1897). Since Marie Heloïse died years before her mother, she could not have succeeded her as Voudou Queen. Plus, it is Marie Philomene who is referenced in the Louisiana Writers' Project interviews, not Marie Heloïse. Marie Philomene Glapion was often referred to as Madame Legendre (alternate spellings Le Jeanne, Lejeune, or Lejuanne) by interviewees.

Figure 4. Marie Laveau and her daughter Marie Philomene Glapion, also known as Madame Legendre. *Credit:* Century Illustrated Magazine, *April 1885*

According to legend, Marie Philomene was a devout Catholic like her mother, but she had no interest in Voudou—and thus was unlikely to be her successor. Nonetheless, if there was indeed a Marie II, it would have to be Marie Philomene, as the date of her death fits the scenario. And, it is said that mother and daughter were very close and lived in the same household, which would mean Marie Philomene was, at the very least, exposed to her mother's Voudou practices; and at most, schooled in them. Furthermore, cloaking Voudou under the guise of Catholicism was something many people did at the time, and we do not know how the social climate changed after her mother's death, which may have necessitated Marie Philomene to be more discreet with her practice.

Described in the *Daily Picayune* (1890) as "a splendid specimen of woman hood" with "large, dark and dreamy eyes that when lit up with excitement, shine with a wonderful light," Marie II was acknowledged as a devoted daughter and pious Catholic. The newspaper went out of its way to make the case that Marie II had no involvement with Voudou and that she "stoutly denies her mother was ever a Voudou Queen or had the least connection with the mystic order." How could she, when "she attended mass daily and was devoted to orphaned children," many of whom she raised herself? This is the same attitude we encounter today by defenders of the Laveau-as-devoted-Catholic legacy, who believe her works of charity could only be due to her Catholic faith and not due to a sense of responsibility to serve her community, a foundational belief of the Voudou religion.

On the other hand, Marie Laveau II is often given credit for being a wild and crazy Voudou Queen like her mother who sacrificed animals and drank their blood in the Louisiana swamps, performed orgiastic rituals, and ran a brothel called the Maison Blanche. She is said to have not been as warm as her mother, and according to an informant interviewed by Tallant by the name of Gerald July, "She was a terrible woman—worse than the first" (Tallant 1946, 62).

All fiction aside, Marie Laveau II was remembered by several informants interviewed by the Louisiana Writers' Project as a pious woman and a good Catholic who had nothing to do with Voudou. Nevertheless, she was reported by a woman named Martha Grey to "make novenas for those in trouble, like the Spiritualists do today. She had an altar with red lamps" (Michinard n.d.). Now, one could make an argument for Voudou activity based on the red lamps comment that may indicate she worked with Petro spirits, which are represented by the color red. In addition, Mami Wata's colors are red and white, so it could be she set lamps to Mami Wata, who I discuss in a later chapter. Lamps are often color coded to correspond with a particular spirit or group of spirits. And Petro spirits are the fiery ones, not necessarily beneficent either, as is implied by Grey's comment. So I would not be so quick to dismiss her involvement in Voudou.

According to lore, Marie Laveau II is said to have drowned in 1897 while crossing the flooded Lake Pontchartrain. On this topic Hurston reports:

> The morning after her death [she] was seen crawling away to the woods about Lake Pontchartrain and was never seen again. There is the story of the storm when she was at her home on the shore of Lake Pontchartrain. She refused to flee, in spite of urging. Finally, the storm swept the cabin into the lake. She resisted rescue, saying that she wished to die there in the lake in the storm. She was always the magnificent savage, and she perhaps felt that, being old, her end was near. She preferred an exit with nature itself playing its most magnificent music than dry rotting in a bed. She was forcibly rescued, but it is said that neither wind, water nor thunder ceased until she had set foot on land (Hurston 1931, 326).

Marie Philomene Glapion lived in the St. Ann Street cottage until she died in 1897. Her children were raised in the Laveau-Glapion home as well. As a side note for Voudou practitioners who acknowledge both mother and daughter as Voudou Queens, Marie Laveau I is referred to as Madame Laveau, while her daughter is referred to as Mademoiselle Laveau. These designations are solely to distinguish mother from daughter in common parlance.

There is a lot more to the second Marie Laveau story, including conflict-ing accounts by authors and scholars as to her identity, her temperament, her activities, and whether or not she was a Voudou priestess. For those interested in the details, I refer you to Carolyn Morrow Long's book, *A New Orleans Voudou Priestess,* where she painstakingly parses through all the literary noise. And although we reach different conclusions as to the second Marie Laveau's identity, it is no wonder there is so much disagreement given the sheer amount of fact mixed with fiction. Long, for example, comes to the conclusion that neither daughter fits the bill for Marie Laveau II and that there wasn't a second Marie Laveau at all. Indeed, I do not deny that possibility. In an interview for the WPA, one woman who was alive during Marie Laveau's lifetime stated when speaking of Marie Laveau, "I never heard of any of her daughters doing that kind of work, and that's the only Marie Laveau I ever saw" (Breaux 1939).

In addition, there may be another explanation for Marie Laveau II, and that would be a case of mistaken identity. For example, Catherine Dillon in her unpublished *Voodoo* manuscript suggested Malvina Latour was actually the Voudou Queen that was presiding over the public rituals attributed to Marie Laveau and newspaper accounts simply got it wrong. Interestingly, I spoke to an individual who indicated their one-hundred-and-one-year-old relative remembers things similarly. She was adamant in her recollections that Malvina Latour was the Voudou Queen and not Marie Laveau at all. I can only surmise that she would be referring to Marie Laveau II and not Marie Catherine Laveau, who we know through the historical record was indeed the Voudou Queen for a period of time. Nonetheless, her account lends anecdotal credence to the case of mistaken identity as suggested by Dillon.

THE DEATH OF THE VOODOO QUEEN

About five years after the death of her husband Christophe, Marie Laveau I became ill and was often bedridden. Her health issues increased as she aged until she was unable to leave her bed at all. According to a newspaper article, she spent her days lying in a "large old-fashioned walnut bedstead, in the front room of the little house which she had never left" (*Staunton Spectator and General Advertiser* 1881). She had decorated her room as one would expect, brimming with sacred pictures and crucifixes, and an altar with wax tapers kept burning day and night. Not only was she dealing with health issues after Christophe's death, she also continued to experience economic hardship, as he left her financially destitute. He died without a will and in a state of insolvency. The Civil War followed his death; these were the social and personal conditions under which she lived out her final years.

Even as the atmosphere changed dramatically from previous years, there was still a ton of activity going on at the Laveau-Glapion home. She continued to allow family members to live there, and she welcomed those in need of food and lodging. She continued to dispense advice and continued practicing the works of mercy. Whatever funds she managed to acquire were shared with others as needed. Contrary to myth, Marie Laveau was not a wealthy woman who made obscene profits off her Voudou business, at least not in her latter years.

In 1886, respected journalist George W. Cable published what is believed to be the last firsthand account of Marie Laveau:

> I once saw, in extreme old age, the famed Marie Laveau . . . she sat quaking with feebleness in an ill-looking old rocking chair, her body bowed, her wild, gray witch's tresses hanging about her shriveled, yellow neck, the queen of the Voodoos. Three generations of her children were within the faint beckon of her helpless, wagging wrist and fingers . . . one could hardly help but see that her face, now so withered, had once been handsome and commanding. There was still a faint shadow of departed beauty in the forehead, the spark of an old fire in the sunken, glistening eyes, and vestige of imperiousness in the fine, slightly aquiline nose, and even about her silent, woebegone mouth . . . Her daughter was also present, a woman of some 70 years, and a most striking and majestic figure.

In features, stature and bearing she was regal. One had but to look at her and impute her brilliances—too untamable and severe to be called charms and graces—to her mother, and remember what New Orleans was long years ago, to understand how the name of Marie Laveau should have driven herself inextricably into the traditions of the town and the times (Cable 1886).

Marie Catherine Laveau died on June 15, 1881, following a long illness at her home on St. Ann Street, with her daughter Marie Philomene Glapion by her side. According to her death certificate, she died from natural causes associated with diarrhea. By all accounts, she was afforded a dignified funeral that was attended by a diverse crowd of people of African, white, and mixed descent, rich and poor alike. She was buried in St. Louis Cemetery No. 1, her body placed in the middle vault with the name Dame Christophe Glapion noted in the ownership records of the tomb (Long 2006). Not long thereafter, her tomb became a popular pilgrimage site among Voudou practitioners and tourists alike.

Two days after her death, the *New Orleans Democrat* printed her obituary. Two other articles were printed three days after her death by the *Daily Picayune* that illustrate stark differences in perceptions of her life and character. Six articles in total were printed about her death.

The Tomb of the Widow Paris

•••

Marie Laveau's final resting place is in a large tomb with a colorful history in St. Louis Cemetery No. 1, the oldest cemetery in the city. Because New Orleans is built on swampland, the Dead cannot be buried in the ground, lest they resurface and float away. Consequently, all but the poor and indigent are laid to rest above ground in elaborate crypts, wall ovens, and mausoleums. Decorative ironwork and sculptures adorn the plots, making the cemeteries resemble little cities; hence the nickname, Cities of the Dead. The cemeteries in New Orleans attract a lot of visitors each year because of their unique, historic character.

St. Louis Cemetery No. 1 is the most famous cemetery in part because of its architecture and history, and in part because Marie Laveau is buried there. When she was alive, people would go to her home on St. Ann Street and knock on her door to ask for help. In death, Voudou adherents from all over the world flock to her tomb for the opportunity to make a wish they hope will be granted by the Voudou Queen.

Referred to as the "Tomb of the Widow Paris," Marie Laveau's grave site is more than just a tourist attraction. It is at the heart of New Orleans' sacred geography. Since her internment in 1881, her tomb has been a powerful liminal space that has evolved over time into a pilgrimage site for devotees from around the world. It connects many sacred spaces running the gamut from swamps to shrines, cemeteries, Congo Square, St. Louis Cathedral, Bayou St. John, and every home where someone lights a candle or says a prayer of devotion to the Voudou Queen. Just as the crossmarks on her tomb mark the point where the physical and spiritual worlds intersect, her tomb

Figure 5. The tomb of Marie Laveau prior to restoration.
Courtesy of Jeffrey Holmes

signifies the place where people from all over the world meet and interact with the spirits of the Dead and the Voodoo Queen herself.

Over the years there has been some disagreement as to whether the Tomb of the Widow Paris is the actual resting place of Marie Laveau. Even though her obituary states that "Marie Laveau was buried in her family tomb in St. Louis Cemetery No. 1," there is an oven wall vault in St. Louis Cemetery No. 2 where locals insist she is buried. According to Carolyn Morrow Long, the "Burial Book states (in English) that 'Dame Christophe Glapion' was placed 'in the family tomb of Vve Paris on June 16, 1881'" (Long 2016, 30). Even with this verified fact that she was interred in the Tomb of the Widow Paris, there remains disagreement as to where she is buried. That shows just how strong the local lore and legend remain.

Figure 6. The Wishing Vault in St. Louis Cemetery No. 2. *Courtesy of Jeffrey Holmes*

Those who reject the Tomb of the Widow Paris as the legitimate resting place for Marie Laveau often cite a local legend that says her family had her body moved from the tomb in St. Louis Cemetery No. 1 to what is referred to as the Wishing Vault in St. Louis Cemetery No. 2. They reportedly did that in order to thwart the attention of tourists and devotees. According to Long (2016), there are no burial records at all for the oven wall vault in St. Louis Cemetery No. 2, so we have no way of knowing who is buried there. Still other legends say she was secretly moved to the Girod St. Cemetery or Holt Cemetery. The 1938 New Orleans City Guide compiled by the Works Progress Administration (WPA) refers to an unmarked grave in St. Louis Cemetery No. 2 this way:

> . . . another supposed resting place of Marie Laveau. The unin-
> scribed concrete is covered with crosses made by the faithful with
> bits of red brick; and devotees still bring contributions of food and

money, especially on St. John's Eve (June 23). Hoodoo money, in two-cent and eleven-cent combinations, left at the base of the tomb will bring good luck to the depositor or bad luck to his enemy. Marie is said to converse with her followers through the walls of her "oven," imparting such information as they desire.

Devotees have been leaving offerings and burning candles at both the St. Louis Cemetery No. 1 and St. Louis Cemetery No. 2 sites for years. In 1898, the *Sun* published an article about two Northern women who had come to New Orleans in search of Marie Laveau's cottage and grave. The two were wandering around the French Quarter with guidebook in hand, searching for the Laveau home. When they found St. Ann Street, they also happened upon a local woman named Marie Smith. Marie shared some colorful stories with them and claimed to have grown up right next door to Marie Laveau. She showed the women the Laveau cottage and then offered to take them to her grave site:

> Dat's a powerful ole house, dat is. Yessum. Dat house is older n my motheh . . . Marie Laveau sho was Injun, yo know. Yessum. Folks thinks she was cullud. Lawd, no! I was brought up right 'longside o' huh an' I know. She was a great woman, sho was. Yo' want me to carry yo' ovoh to St. Louis Cem'tery an' show you where she's buried?
>
> The two Northern women said they would be delighted to be "carried" over to the cemetery . . . a few days later, they hunted up Marie for the promised trip to the cemetery. She "carried" them over, as agreed, to old St. Louis Cemetery, one of the landmarks of the old quarter. It is crowded with whitewashed tombs ten or twelve feet high, with tablets in front. Marie took her two travellers around to one of the best of the tombs and there triumphantly pointed out the Inscription (*Sun* 1898).

Once upon a time, travelers could visit her tomb on any day of the year to leave offerings, make wishes, and pay homage to the Voudou Queen. Tour guides began bringing sightseers there during the 1980s and, blessed

Figure 7. Offerings left at the tomb of the Widow Paris. *Courtesy of Russell Hamel*

with the gift of gab, many a story emerged from their colorful tales. All this changed, however, on December 24, 2013, when renowned occult author Dorothy Morrison wrote this on Facebook:

> As grand a time as we're having in New Orleans, we did make a rather disturbing discovery this morning: Someone painted Marie Laveau's tomb . . . I can hardly bring myself to say this . . . pastel PINK!!! WTF??? Someone local: Please find out who did this and make them change it back! It's disgusting, and I don't think Madame is very happy about it.

A flurry of responses and reactions ensued, as you may well imagine. Most people expressed disdain, but a few did not find the color objectionable. "PINK!? OOOO SHEEET! Madam Laveau just got a barrio-style touch up!" said Absolem Yetzirah of Societe Bayou Ville, a temple dedicated to the service of Marie Laveau in Houston, Texas. He went on to state that he rather liked the color because it reminded him of the colorful tombs in some of the Mexican Catholic cemeteries. "What is the color pink in conjure work?" he asked. "Pink is associated with friendship, honor, love, morality, affection, spiritual awakening, unselfishness, leadership, femininity, togetherness, unity and healing . . . In the barrio traditions, pink is used to generate great affection. This is why you will see many tombs of grandmothers and mothers painted pink in the valley cemeteries" (Absolem Yetzirah, personal communication, December 24, 2013).

Even though the Archdiocese of New Orleans owns and operates St. Louis Cemetery No. 1, where the tomb of the Widow Paris is located, they did not routinely maintain the tomb. Most of the tombs in the cemetery are individually owned by families, who are ultimately responsible for their maintenance and upkeep. If there is no family, there is no upkeep. It is estimated that 75 percent of almost one thousand tombs in St. Louis Cemetery No. 1 are orphaned. According to archdiocesan records, Marie Laveau's last known family member was buried in 1957, and since then no one has been responsible for taking care of the tomb. As a result, Save Our Cemeteries, the Archdiocese of New Orleans, and Bayou Preservation, LLC formed a partnership to restore the tomb. Nearly a year later, the restoration of the Voodoo Queen's tomb was completed and unveiled on Halloween day, 2014.

Since it's restoration, the primary concern was to prevent the same sort of inadvertent destruction of the tomb from occurring in the future. Some suggested partitioning the tomb off from the public altogether. As with all things Laveau, there are stories. One such story is recounted by Jack Barrett: "I don't know how much is true, but there's a story of a NOLA city councilman who wanted her tomb cordoned off with no public access, and who woke up one morning with his bedroom full of snakes. After that, he would encounter a cottonmouth everywhere he went, even finding them in his refrigerator" (Jack Barrett, personal communication, April 2019). Partitioning the tomb off was a wildly unpopular idea and instead the decision was made to make the cemetery no longer open access. If you wish to visit Marie Laveau's tomb, you must now be accompanied by a tour guide in order to do so.

CROSSMARKS

At some point not long after her death, people began petitioning Marie Laveau at her grave site by marking her tomb with three crossmarks (*XXX*) using broken red bricks from nearby graves and leaving offerings at the base of the tomb. One interesting custom was recounted in 1931 by the cemetery sexton: "Nice looking young ladies come" he said. "They pass down that way . . . and before every tomb they stop and tap three times while they whisper the wish they want to come true. Then they come to the Voodoo tomb and say the wish out loud" (*The Miami News* 1931). In 1936, the *Pensacola News Journal* reported "Men, women and children call secretly at the grave" on St. John's Eve "to use this means to establish contact with Marie and obtain favors."

Critics have stated the drawing of crossmarks is not a traditional Voudou practice, and blame has been placed on the tourist industry for what has been deemed a destructive practice. While it is unknown who started the practice, the act of signing with a crossmark is called *kwasiyen* in Haitian Vodou. It signifies a point of power, a liminal space where the

Figure 8. Crossmarks on the Tomb of the Widow Paris. *Courtesy of Jeffrey Holmes*

world of the Visibles and Invisibles meet and is used to establish communication with the Dead and the loa. While most people are unaware of the origins of the practice and simply emulate what they see, Marie Laveau was known to draw three crossmarks on the ground in front of graves when doing her conjure work, so perhaps the tradition actually comes from the Voudou Queen herself.

Originally, the crossmarks on Marie Laveau's grave were made with soft red bricks from nearby crumbling graves, so they were a characteristic brick red in color. Over time, however, people began making crossmarks in different colors. The colors of the crossmarks would point to the nature of the petition made. According to one tour guide:

> The white X is a general wish. . . . The blue X is for good health, yellow is for luck, purple is for courage and strength, brown is for definite favors and red is generic. . . . But the black X is the bad one—it's for putting a hex on someone, and that's frowned upon (Miller 1994, 14).

The passion with which many devotees feel entitled to inscribe crossmarks on the Widow Paris tomb is fierce. According to one person I spoke to, putting small crossmarks on her tomb is an act of devotion, not defacement. Another individual stated it is a way of honoring her. Nevertheless, the act of drawing on a tomb is considered desecration and is, in fact, illegal.

THE WISHING RITUAL

As far back as I can remember, the practice of drawing three crossmarks on Marie Laveau's tomb was referred to as the "Wishing Ritual." The ritual has always had some variations on a theme, but the manner in which I am familiar is to approach her tomb and give her a few compliments about her strength, intelligence, and beauty, and acknowledge her as Voudou Queen. Then, knock on the tomb three times. In the past, you would write three crossmarks with red brick on her tomb, but nowadays you can just make the gesture with your finger. Next, make your petition and ask her for what you want. Thank her and go to St. Louis Cathedral and light a candle. Leave a donation to really get in her good graces.

If you approach Marie Laveau's tomb and make a wish and it comes true, it used to be customary to return to her grave site with flowers and other offerings to thank her. However, leaving offerings at the tomb is no longer allowed. Therefore, one way to get around leaving a physical offering at the time of petitioning her is to make a donation to charity via your mobile phone while there. This means you will have to prepare; decide which charity you wish to donate to and pull it up on your cell phone before going to visit so you can do it quickly. Alternately, make your donation ahead of time and tell her that you did so in preparation of your visit and request for assistance.

To have access to the Wishing Tomb at all times without actually being there, I came up with an alternate act of devotion years ago. First, put an image of her tomb in a frame and set it on her altar. Using red lipstick, mark three crossmarks on the tomb side by side (*XXX*). Knock on the photo three times and ask Marie Laveau to grant your wish. For example: "Beautiful Marie Laveau, miracle worker of the courts, please see that the judge rules in my favor." Then turn around three times clockwise, light a blue candle, and make an offering of fresh flowers, coconut cake, or fruit. When your wish comes true, wipe off the crossmarks and clean the frame as if tidying up her grave. Thank Marie Laveau and make a donation to charity in her honor.

Another option for devotees to perform the wishing ritual is to visit the International Shrine of Marie Laveau located in the New Orleans Healing Center on St. Claude Avenue. Just inside the lobby is a shrine of Marie Laveau. New Orleans artist Ricardo Pustanio created the statue and donated it to Mambo Sallie Ann Glassman of La Source Ancienne Ounfo. A great community alternative to visiting her grave site, people leave little slips of paper and light candles at the shrine. The shrine was formally installed with a mosaic tile created via contributions from the community during a blessing ceremony at the Sacred Music Festival in March 2015.

Figure 9. The International Shrine of Marie Laveau.
Courtesy of Sallie Ann Glassman

Laveau Voudou:
A New Religion

•••

There was always a line of carriages in front of Marie's house, and the ladies who entered the house were heavily veiled. The women of the elite of New Orleans did not hesitate to go and consult Marie Laveau, who would give them powders to use on their husbands, and bones and skeletons to put in their pockets.

—MIMI DALAVIGNE[4]

In Louisiana, Voudou is almost always associated with Marie Laveau. She is the Voudou Queen of New Orleans, quite literally. She took the traditions of her ancestors—along with her mother's and her grandmother's flair for entrepreneurship—and found a way to harmoniously blend the Catholic religion imposed upon her with her indigenous Creole practices. And she made a little money in the process! She triumphantly traversed both Catholic and Voudou worlds and was accepted, for the most part, by the society in which she lived.

Marie Laveau's successful combination of Catholic elements, African religions, and Creole culture survived more than one hundred and fifty years and is carried on and emulated to this day by devotees and practitioners alike. Thus, her style of Voudou has proven persistent and worthy of acknowledgment as a definitive, emergent Creole tradition. But because there are so many different expressions of New Orleans Voudou, and because not everyone embraces her or Catholicism in their practice, I call Marie Laveau's brand of New Orleans Voudou *Laveau Voudou* to differentiate it from other forms of Creole Voudou in Louisiana.

To understand Laveau Voudou, we must first understand the basics of Voudou in general. The word *Voudou* means "spirit of God." West African

Vodun cosmology centers on the *vodun*—the spirits and other elements of divine essence that govern the Earth. It is a religious system often called monotheistic, but that term is not accurate. It is more precisely described as henotheistic, because it acknowledges the existence of one ultimate God but does not deny there are other deities as well. To illustrate, New Orleans Voudou is based on a hierarchy of spirits consisting of three levels: at the top, Bon Dieu (Good God); below that are powerful spirits referred to as loas and orishas; and third are the Ancestors. In addition, saints, angels, spirit guides, and revered cultural heroes are also acknowledged. These powerful spirits act as intermediaries between Bon Dieu and humans and assist us in the daily matters of life. They love us, guard us, and protect us. They give us solutions to our problems. All of the spirits help us navigate life, warning us of impending danger while ripping the masks off those who would wish us harm. Finally, Ancestor reverence is considered to be the foundation of New Orleans Voudou. The loas, orishas, and Ancestors are not worshipped; rather, they are served and revered, respectively.

There are three primary forms of Voudou in New Orleans: African Vodun, Haitian Vodou, and New Orleans Voudou. There are varying degrees of overlap among them and colloquially speaking, all of these forms fall under the umbrella term *Voudou* in Louisiana. New Orleans Voudou consists of numerous expressions due to its folk status, survival among families, appeal to the individual practitioner, and, "Because many 'Louisiana Voodoo' practitioners are fearful of ostracism, ridicule, and further persecution, they have become a type of 'underground' religion in New Orleans" (Maranise 2012, 2). Elmer Glover, a New Orleans bokor, stated during a panel discussion in 2011 called *Vaudou Practice in Haiti and New Orleans*, "There are different types of Voudou. We have what is called Ifá, Orisha, Lukumi, Santeria, Umbanda, and ancient Egyptian practices to name a few. All of these are forms of Voudou." Voudou Priestess Claudia Williams from Starling Magickal in New Orleans and keeper of the official shrine to Doctor John Montenee stated, "I grew up with the teaching that all African Traditional Religions fell under the umbrella term 'Vodou' or 'Voodoo.' Everyone's teaching varies slightly" (Claudia Williams, personal communication April 19, 2019).

Speaking with and listening to New Orleanians, the concept of individual expression in their Voudou practice becomes very clear. Mambo Mary Millan, also known as Bloody Mary in New Orleans, writes on her website that "New Orleans Voodoo Queen Marie Laveau was very influential on the spiritualist movement and as a spirit guide of our House and New Orleans Séance Parlor, her shrine watches over." Additionally, Priestess Claudia states, "Personally, I don't see how a New Orleans Vodou practitioner could possibly NOT love Marie Laveau. To me, she is in most ways the originator of this area of Vodou. Not that Vodou hadn't been here, but she and Dr. John put a real 'American' imprint on it" (Claudia Williams, personal communication April 19, 2019). According to Mambo Sallie Ann Glassman, "I consider Marie to be a revered Ancestor and is becoming a lwa. Especially in the last few years, witnessing the quality of reverence, respect, appreciation and awe people bring to her at the Healing Center shrine, how people make pilgrimages from all over the world just to be in her presence and the numerous thank you notes and plaques attesting to the many miracles she performs in her life, I believe she is elevating to the level of lwa" (Sallie Ann Glassman, personal communication February 22, 2019). At the same time, Priestess Miriam of the Voodoo Spiritual Temple in New Orleans relates she does not follow a rigid method for performing public ceremonies or private rituals, because it can be spiritually and creatively stifling. In addition, 'following a script,' as she phrases it, can prevent people from experiencing and understanding what the Spirit is trying to convey" (Bilinsky 2016, 54).

While most New Orleans Voudou practitioners serve and work with Marie Laveau in some capacity, either as loa, spirit guide, or elevated Ancestor, there exists another form of New Orleans Voudou practiced by those who do not like Marie Laveau because of her commercialization of the religion. As a result, these individuals refer to their form of New Orleans Voudou simply as "The Religion" and their members as the Faithful (Osbey 2011). These individuals are not Marie Laveau devotees and do not include her as a spirit in their service to the Ancestors.

CREOLIZATION

Culture itself, and the traditions that emerge from it, is dynamic; it is not static or fixed. Culture preserves traditions, but also possesses mechanisms for change (Fieldhouse 1988). Creolization is the mechanism by which immigrants, migrants, and indigenous populations who live in close proximity emerge as a blended, new, Creole culture. Each population has something to contribute, including art, food, music, and folk beliefs. Within the context of a culturally pluralistic society, creolization enables the formation of new identities, including the emergence of new religions. Louisiana hosted a large population of enslaved individuals from a variety of regions in Africa whose traditions, coupled with the indigenous influences in the Americas and European folk traditions, resulted in a religiomagickal and spiritual atmosphere rich with mysteries. Thus, New Orleans Voudou, and by extension Laveau Voudou, can only be truly understood as a collective of religiomagickal systems of meaning that is by its very nature fluid. Using this framework, we can see how it developed from a primarily African, indigenous tradition to the fully creolized religion it is today.

As it stands, Laveau Voudou is a new tradition that emerged in the New World from the process of creolization while under the influence of the Louisiana Black Code. It originated from the ancestral religions of the African Diaspora and over time there was an assimilation of deities and practices from the various religious and cultural traditions into a new and unique American Creole Voudou. There are distinct contributions from the Congo region, such as the phenomenon of working with spirits in buckets and cauldrons (e.g., Ancestor pots, Black Hawk's bucket, and Marie Laveau's cauldron), as well as talismanic magick brought to the Americas by the Bambara (e.g., gris gris), and Yoruba deities such as Eshu/Elegba and Ogun (Fandrich 2007). After the United States purchased the Louisiana Territory in 1803, there were several influxes of immigrants from San Domingue who brought with them their version of Caribbean Vodou and their own pantheon of spirits. Enmeshed in all of the above is Catholicism, which was the legally mandated religion in New Orleans. Aspects of some of the religions and traditions stuck, while others didn't. This is completely natural and expected in such circumstances.

When I use the term Creole Voudou, I intend for it to cover all of the various forms of Voudou in Louisiana. New Orleans Voudou and Laveau Voudou are both forms of Creole Voudou, yet they differ in significant ways. Laveau Voudou acknowledges and serves Marie Laveau as a revered Ancestor and loa. Laveau devotees also embrace elements of Catholicism as central to the practice. On the other hand, practitioners of New Orleans Voudou may or may not acknowledge and serve Marie Laveau with the same degree of importance. Furthermore, New Orleans Voudouists may or may not be practicing Catholics. Louis Martinié, Spiritual Elder and ritual drummer with the Voodoo Spiritual Temple, states that some New Orleans Voudouists are atheists—some believe in a Christian God and some do not. I have found this to be true as well but saying this out loud makes you no friends. Martinié further states the religion is not standardized and "there is no central organization to propose and impose orthodoxy of expression" (Martinié 2010, 20).

Today, Voudou in New Orleans is taking on a stronger Haitian flavor due to the increasing number of people moving to New Orleans who are already initiated in Haitian Vodou. At least half of the commercial Voudou and conjure sector appear to be new to New Orleans as a result of Hurricane Katrina. As the congregations grow under the Mambos and Houngans, more people are being initiated into Haitian Vodou and the traditional rites of New Orleans Voudou and her Queens are at risk of disappearing. This fact makes the publication of books such as this one extremely important in documenting forms of the tradition that have heretofore gone undocumented because they have been unknown to outsiders. It is important to preserve our folk traditions given the history and sacrifice behind family lines of Voudou and out of respect for our Voudou Queen.

VOUDOU VERSUS HOODOO

An issue of note to folks mostly from outside of our tradition is the conflation of Voudou and Hoodoo. During the latter part of the 1800s, the two terms were used interchangeably. No one knows when this began to happen or why. There are a few theories, mostly by white authors who posit African Americans mistakenly began calling Hoodoo Voudou or vice versa. Others say it was white folks who began calling Voudou Hoodoo or vice versa. I truly believe this is not an issue to Marie Laveau or her followers, as she clearly engaged in Voudou rituals, magick, and gris gris and did not develop illusory categories to define what she was doing. New Orleans practitioners follow suit, rarely arguing this point amongst themselves as we understand how the various aspects of the tradition originated in different regions of Africa and came together in a beautiful, hybridized blend.

On the other hand, Hoodoo can stand alone as a magickal tradition, so it may or may not be embraced by Voudou practitioners. That said, an informant in Harry Middleton Hyatt's *Hoodoo-Conjuration-Witchcraft-Rootwork* responded to Hyatt's question, "Is there any difference between Hoodoo and Voodoo?" with "No difference as ah see it. Dey seem to be the same thing" (Hyatt 1970, 1:949). This same informant discusses Hoodoo as working with roots and powders while the other—which she describes as "Spiritualist"—works with the spirits. She does not go out of her way to describe Voudou and Hoodoo as mutually exclusive until asked a specific leading line of questioning by Hyatt. Additionally, in an 1893 article, *The Buffalo Enquirer* describes both terms thus:

> "Voudou," as the French-speaking people of New Orleans call it, or "Hoodoo," as the term is known among others, is synonymous with superstitious terrors of malevolence, sickness brought about by uncanny influences and terrible infirmities, the result of satanic incantations, helped by the use of powders and compound drugs of alleged extraordinary potency.

In sum, the best way I can clarify the relationship between Hoodoo and Voudou in Louisiana is that some people Hoodoo, and some people don't. Voudouists who Hoodoo do not have any issues embracing it as part of their Voudou practice anymore than they have a problem with working gris gris. As a Creole tradition, we understand it is the very nature of being Creole to embrace every aspect of our culture and have little desire to dissect it for the sake of comforting the cognitive dissonance expressed by outsiders.

INFLUENCE OF THE VOUDOU QUEEN

Though we have no evidence to inform us how and when Marie Laveau started practicing Voudou, it is suspected she began her career as a Voudou Queen sometime in the 1820s. According to oral history, she was mentored by the already established Voudou Priestesses at the time, Sanité Dédé and Marie Saloppé. It is also shared cultural knowledge that she worked at least for a period of time with Doctor John Montenee learning the art of gris gris. Doctor John, also known as Bayou John, did very well for himself and made quite a bit of money as an herbalist and fortune teller. He owned several properties and is said to have run a brothel. He couldn't read or write, though he did learn to sign his name, thanks to an alleged friend who taught him. One day, the friend showed Doctor John a piece of paper and had him sign his name on the paper. Unknowingly, he signed away the deeds to his properties. He had been hoodwinked and lost everything.

Even as he had a reputation for being an effective "Indian doctor"—a term used at the time to identify herbal healers as medicine men whether or not they were actually Native American—Doctor John was also a player. He had several wives and is said to have disliked all but African women. "He was negro to the core, in color, origin and principle" writes Henry Castellanos for the *Times Democrat* in 1894. "A mulatto was his special aversion. 'Too black to be white,' he was wont to say, 'and too white to be black, the fellow is a hybrid and a mule.'" Knowing the kind of woman Marie Laveau was, I can imagine she got tired of his shenanigans and parted ways to build her own following and congregation. It should be noted that there is no written evidence showing any ties between Doctor John and Marie Laveau, yet it is a significant piece of oral history.

As the most influential Voudou Queen in New Orleans' history, there is no doubt that Marie Laveau was a driving force in the formation of New Orleans Voudou in four distinct ways. First, she incorporated Catholic elements into her practice such as saints, Psalms, and candle magick. She used swaths of incense in her rituals and included Mary in her pantheon. She practiced the works of mercy with her charitable works and prison ministry. She combined standard Catholic liturgical prayers with Voudou songs and prayers in her rites and held annual Voudou fetes on St. John's Eve and St. John's Night. And, she treated her gris gris like holy relics, blessed by the gods and possessed with magickal properties of removing evil influences and bringing about positive or negative change.

Evidence of Marie Laveau's blending of Catholic elements alongside Voudou was noted throughout her lifetime. "Side by side in the room of the Voudou Queen," writes one reporter, "on the same table as the serpent, was the cross of the crucified Savior, the image of Virgin Mary, and various symbols of saints and angels" (*Times Daily Picayune* 1890, 10). Reports of the recital of the Apostles' Creed, Hail Mary, and Ave Marie Stella at the beginning of Voudou ceremonies were also observed, a practice that continues today as a New Orleans Voudou Order of Service.

The second way in which Marie Laveau as Voudou Queen had a lasting affect on Voudou in Louisiana involves her ritual space. Marie's activities centered around specific places in and around New Orleans and as a result, these places have become significant points on the sacred geography of New Orleans. Congo Square, Bayou St. John, and Lake Pontchartrain are some of the places that she is associated with for performing public dances and ceremonies. W. W. Newell reported, "The festivals of the 'Vaudous' were supposed to be annual, and to take place at a lonely spot near Lake Pontchartrain, on St. John's Eve" (Newell 1889). In 1937, the *Daily Independent* wrote, "Marie Laveau and her followers went into the swamps and performed their mystic rites." And, in 1898 the *Sun* wrote, "At one time Marie Laveau was the Queen of the famous Voudoos, who held their strange rites and dances in Congo Square."

Clearly, the most popular of all the public Voudou celebrations was the annual celebration of St. John's Eve, the Holy Day of New Orleans Voudou. It is one of the only feast days in Catholicism that celebrates the birth of a saint: St. John the Baptist. The only other two whose births are celebrated are Jesus and Mary. Usually, feast days celebrate the deaths of saints. In New Orleans, St. John's Eve and St. John's Day are now the days for celebrating the Mother and Father of New Orleans Voudou, Marie Laveau and Doctor John Montenee.

Bayou St. John was one of the spots where Marie Laveau held her annual St. John's Eve ceremony; but, that's not the only thing it is known for. One belief tied to the Laveau legend holds that if a person has been crossed, they can remove the conjure by submerging themselves in the spot where Marie Laveau II reportedly drowned. Another bit of lore is the Wishing Spot located on the lakeside of Bayou St. John at the intersection of DeSaix Blvd. There was a hollow tree trunk that functioned like a wishing well where people tossed coins and dollar bills and burned candles in the hopes their wishes would be answered. In another hallowed-out tree in Congo Square referred to as the Wishing Tree, Marie was known for leaving plates of jambalaya and money for the needy after her public dances held there.

The third way Marie Laveau influenced Voudou in New Orleans was by making a business out of her practice. Indeed, "She had the brains of an Executive of Big Business in planning, organizing, directing" (*St. Louis Post Dispatch* 1933). People of all races went to her for help with matters of daily living. Court cases, relationship issues, money problems, and employment were among the common areas of life that she was known to be of assistance. Women of high society paid good sums for her amulets designed to bring good luck, while "politicians and candidates for office were known to purchase their 'mascots' at her fortune shop" and "sporting men would wear, attached to their watch chains, pieces of bone or wood, fantastically carved" (*Times Democrat* 1894). She had people working for her as well, and between her networking, contacts, and positions as hairdresser, healer, and priestess, she was able to understand what her clients needed:

> So large a number voluntarily came and confided in her that she became mistress of the secrets of many families—for the most influential families will have secrets, the discovery of which they own dread. This knowledge and her own shrewdness were the mystery of her power, just as they are of the power of others who lay claim to supernatural influence. As was to be expected in such a woman, she was discreet. Her secrets died with her. What she knew was the unwritten history of New Orleans—more interesting and far more startling than any which has been told (*Times Picayune* 1886).

Of course, not everyone was a fan of Marie's. It is said that some were hellbent on exposing her evil deeds but dared not because it was believed that should anyone cross her in that way, "she would publish a list of names of everybody who went to her" (Breaux 1939).

Lastly, Marie Laveau embraced the Temple snakes in her service. According to Martinié, the Temple snakes, Damballah and Ayida Wedo, "are central to the liturgies of the New Orleans Voodoo Spiritual Temple" (Martinié, 2010, 78). Li Grand Zombi was both the name of her personal temple snake, as well as the term referencing all of the temple snakes in her tradition. The etymology of the word *Zombi* derives from the Kongo Bantu word *Nzambi,* meaning *God* in the Kikongo language (Fandrich 2007, 786). Thus, Li Grand Zombi signifies a direct connection to the serpent religious traditions of West Africa and the African creator deity Nzambi.

MARIE LAVEAU'S SPIRITUAL COURT

Though African in origin, Marie Laveau's style of Voudou, "while still retaining the ancient characteristics of the Congo belief, developed into a curious mingling of refined faith and spiritualism" (*Times Daily Picayune*

1890). When we talk about a spiritual court, we are referring to a group of spirits that surround each person. This is a concept common to several of the African-derived traditions. While there is no way to ascertain with absolute certainty all of the spirits that comprised Marie Laveau's personal spiritual court, we do have some references to specific saints and African deities in association with her. For example, there are references to St. Peter, St. Anthony, St. John the Baptist, St. Michael, Mami Wata, St. Maroon, Li Grand Zombi, Damballah Wedo, and the Spirit of Death. If we take syncretism into consideration, St. Peter is associated with Papa Legba, as both hold the keys to the kingdom of heaven—or in Legba's case, the Visible and Invisible worlds. St. Peter and Papa Legba are invoked at the beginning of traditional Hoodoo ceremonies of the parterre variety, as well as at the public Voudou ritual dances. Historically in New Orleans Voudou, you may petition St. Peter in place of Papa Legba, in addition to Papa Legba, or as Papa Legba. If discretion is of the utmost concern, then the last alternative is ideal.

Interestingly, we hear nothing in the historical records referring to the terms *loa* and *orisha* as it relates to New Orleans Voudou. We do hear the term *spirits,* and this is a term that continues to be favored in Louisiana. I believe the term *loa* (spelled *lwa* in reference to Haitian Vodou) likely arrived with the Haitians when they came to New Orleans. During the eighteenth and nineteenth centuries, we also don't hear much in the way of the pantheon of spirits simply because practitioners were not the ones writing about their traditions back then. What we have in the historical record are accounts of observers, very often misinformed, so their characterizations were generalizations at best. Most of the time, reporters covering Voudou activities had no idea what they were looking at. The descriptions they gave, however, do provide clues about what spirits and practices were part of the various ceremonies and rituals. Following are brief descriptions of some of the spirits described by witnesses of Laveau Voudou ceremonies in the 1800s.

Damballah Wedo

Damballah Wedo is one of the most revered of the African gods, the serpent deity of peace and purity, of platinum and silver, and the one who grants riches and sustains the world. Optimism emanates from his presence, and it is he who is the original servant to the Creator. Damballah is an ancient loa, referred to as a "root" loa. Damballah is syncretized with St. Patrick and Moses.

> Damballah Wedo was also called as the great Voodoo Queen stood up and holding up her snake Zombi over her head chanted: 'Damballah—Ye—Ye—Ye!' three times. The drums as usual beat with an increasing tempo. Damballah Wedo brings together the most powerful aspects of the male and female loas as one (Gandolfo 1992, 23).

Damballah's partner is Ayida Wedo, the rainbow serpent. Though she is not mentioned in any nineteenth- or twentieth-century reports associated with Marie Laveau, it is common practice in New Orleans Voudou to serve the partner of a loa when known. Therefore, in New Orleans Voudou, Damballah and Ayida Wedo are always served together—the serpent and the rainbow.

Baron Samedi

Baron Samedi is the Voudou loa of Death and head of the ancestral loa called the Guede. Baron Samedi is considered one of the patron loas of New Orleans, as he stands at the crossroads where the souls of dead humans pass on their way to Guinee. He is noted for disruption, obscenity, and debauchery, and for having a particular fondness for tobacco (especially Pall Mall cigarettes), money, and white rum. He is a very powerful magician and is helpful with magick rituals, especially those involving children, money, and life changes. Further, he is the only spirit who can determine who lives and who dies. Baron Samedi is known to be very wise and honest in his responses to those seeking his help.

While not explicitly called by name in rituals described by reporters and witnesses of Marie Laveau's magick, I believe he may have been represented. In her gris gris ceremonies, Marie Laveau always summoned Li Grand Zombi; but in one description, she also called upon the Spirit of Death: "She summoned the spirits of darkness and death, the supreme power of the great Zombi, who protects and hears the Voudoo's prayer" when suddenly, "there appeared in the group the Voudoo, being clad in the garb of death . . . he wore a skull and crossbones upon his bosom and carried a scythe in one hand and a small wooden coffin in the other" (*Times Daily Picayune* 1890, 10). A ritual is then described whereby the Spirit of Death knelt in front of the serpent and knocked on the ground three times. Grabbing a rag doll from the altar, he placed it into the little coffin along with a handful of dirt gathered from the ground—more than likely grave dirt. Once he closed the coffin, it signaled the point of the ceremony when all of the participants approached the gris gris pot and received their portion, and the Dance of Death, known today as the Banda, commenced.

Calling upon Baron Samedi for making magick is consistent with what we know about him and his role in Voudou. He is associated with a type of death conjure called *l'envoi morts,* or *Expéditions,* meaning "Sending of the Dead" (Métraux 1959). Expéditions are a type of death curse that when performed resemble the Marie Laveau ceremony. The bokor knocks three times on the ground using a machete, provides offerings, and uses grave dirt in the conjure.

Baron Samedi remains a popular and powerful force in New Orleans Voudou today, along with his wife Manman Brigit. He is syncretized with St. Expedite, among the most popular of saints in New Orleans. We do not hear of St. Expedite in association with Marie Laveau, however, because he did not achieve popularity until the late 1800s or early 1900s in New Orleans (Alvarado 2014).

Li Grand Zombi

No doubt a holdover from Dahomey, where serpent worship was a part of the original Vodun religion, the power of the snake both as a primary deity and as a powerful animal who possesses strong magick is an integral aspect of the New Orleans Voudou religion and central to Laveau Voudou. It is well known that Marie Laveau had a snake that she called *Zombi* and that she danced with this snake during her rituals with her congregation. Some say she kept the snake in a box at the foot of her bed; other accounts say it was under the bed; and still another account claims that she didn't have a snake at all, but kept a jointed wooden snake on her altar to fool superstitious people (Puckett 1926).

There are different reports as to the species of snake held by Marie Laveau. Some say it was "the harmless, nonvenomous Louisiana king-snake, often six feet long, with black skin and greenish-grey like candle grease drippings" that "became the convenient symbol of Gran Zombi" (*St. Louis Post Dispatch* 1933). Castellano described "a box containing the god's manifestation—an enormous moccasin snake heaped upon itself in loathsome folds." In another newspaper article, Li Grand Zombi was "Usually represented by a long black Congo eel or the deadly cottonmouth" (*Daily World* 1957). Today, it is generally believed it was a boa constrictor or python. Whatever may be the case, the name *Li Grand Zombi* refers not only to Marie Laveau's personal serpent familiar, but also serpents as a whole in New Orleans Voudou:

> The Grand Zombie assumes myriad functions and forms in New Orleans Voudou. It is the sacred snake in its widest sense. The Grande Zombie can act as a singular loa, or, in another sense, "Grande Zombie" can act as a blanket term covering all of the snake loa of New Orleans Voudou" (Martinié 2010).

Mami Wata

Indeed, we find a clue historically to another African deity connection on August 16, 1820, when the *Louisiana Gazette* reported a police raid on a Faubourg Tremé home in New Orleans. Among those arrested were several free people of color, some slaves, and a single white man. The site of the raid was used for late-night gatherings of a religious, albeit illegal, nature, a home "used as a temple for certain occult practices and the idolatrous worship of an African deity called Vaudoo" (*Louisiana Gazette* 1820). Ritual objects were also confiscated, including "the image of a woman, whose lower extremities resemble a snake"

Figure 10. Sculpture of the African water deity Mami Wata. Nigeria (Igbo). 1950s. Wood, pigment. Original in the Minneapolis Institute of Art.

(*Louisiana Gazette* 1820). From that brief description, the image sounds like Mami Wata, aka Mami Waters, meaning Mother Water, who was brought to Louisiana by way of enslaved peoples of West Africa (Benin, Togo, and Ghana).

Mami Wata is depicted as a mermaid, with a woman's torso and the legs of either a fish or serpent. Sometimes Mami Wata is depicted as a whole woman carrying a large snake or snakes wrapped around her body. While she is often depicted as a mermaid or half woman–half snake, Mami Wata actually represents a whole pantheon of spirits and deities in West Africa. Mami Wata is the African ambassador to all the spirits of the waters: La Sirene, the Haitian Vodou loa who is similarly depicted as a mermaid; Yemoja, the Yoruban Mother of the Seven Seas; and Yemayá in Santeria and Ifá. Mami Wata remains an important spirit in the New Orleans Voudou pantheon.

There is another documented incidence of a large wooden fetish that was likely Mami Wata. Referred to as the Voudou Virgin by the press, the fetish was reportedly confiscated by the police on August 10, 1850. This time, a gathering of Voudous was once again raided, and in the process several ritual items were seized. Among the items taken by the police was a wooden statue, a "chief relic of reverence and veneration . . . a quaintly carved wooden figure, resembling something between a Centaur and an Egyptian Mummy" (*Daily Delta* 1850). The newspapers called it the "Virgin of the Voudous." The fact that they called it a virgin indicates it was likely female, and the reference to a centaur signals it was half woman-half creature in appearance. These clues, coupled with the previous 1820 report, lead me to believe the Voudou Virgin was a Mami Wata statue.

While confiscating items at a raid is common practice by the police, it quickly became evident that taking the Voudou Virgin was a big deal and that it would have to be returned to the Voudou community. After keeping it locked up with contraband for a period of time, and following several failed attempts by folks in the community to get the fetish back, a rumor started floating around that the police officer in possession of the fetish would sell it to the first Voudou woman to pay him $8.50. In no time at all, "the first one to reach the police was a young quadroon who paid the stated ransom and retired with her precious burden" (Dillard Project 1942, 36). She was followed by a number of other practitioners, each seeking possession of the most powerful, magickal fetish in New Orleans at the time, some offering two to three times the amount initially requested. Members of the Voudou community were upset it had been snatched up so quickly, so they decided to take the matter to the courts.

On the day of the court proceedings, at about 11 in the morning, a whole slew of folks showed up to make the case for their rightful owner-ship of the Voudou Virgin. Despite having good representation and putting forth their best arguments, in the end the judge ruled the fetish should stay in the possession of the quadroon who initially purchased it.

Of course, nothing is as straightforward as it seems in the life and legend of Marie Laveau. A different version of this very incident is provided by Herbert Asbury in his book, *The French Quarter,* wherein he describes a quadroon named Rosalie who had set her sights on overthrowing Marie Laveau as Queen of the Voudous. Apparently, Rosalie was in possession of a very powerful magickal fetish she had imported directly from Africa, "an almost life-size doll which had been carved from a single tree-trunk" (Asbury 1936, 265). The magickal fetish was invariably coveted by all the Voudous as it represented the Mother Land, life before slavery, and the origin of the Voudou mysteries:

> Painted in brilliant colors and bedecked in beads and gaudy ribbons, this doll formed such an impressive spectacle, and was so obviously a source of magick, that Rosalie began to make considerable headway in her schemes of rebellion (Asbury 1936, 265).

Once Marie Laveau got wind of Rosalie's plans, she went to Rosalie's home when she wasn't there, marched right inside, grabbed the fetish, and left "in a characteristically masterful manner" (Asbury 1936, 265). Removing the object of power from Rosalie immediately removed any edge she may have had over Marie. This bold act put Rosalie back where she belonged, under the influence of the Voudou Queen, like everyone else.

But Rosalie wasn't going to relinquish her power so easily. She actually had Marie Laveau arrested and took her to court! Clearly, Marie had stolen the fetish but from a magickal perspective, she had to in order to retain power.

And as to be expected, Marie absolutely maintained her power. She presented such a convincing case to the judge he actually ruled in her favor! Marie was allowed to keep the fetish, and "possession of this potent fetish, together with a magick shawl which she said had been sent to her by the Emperor of China in 1830, made her authority secure" (Asbury 1936, 266).

As a side note, the Egyptian mummy part of the Voudou Virgin description points to the possibility that the fetish could have been an African power object characteristic of the Congo called a *nkisi*. The description of the doll "bedecked in beads and gaudy ribbons" sounds like these types of ritual objects as they typically have strips of fabric attached to them along with beads and a variety of other items. They really resemble assemblage art, and indeed every item attached to the object has a supernatural meaning and intention behind it. The strips of fabric may call to mind a mummy.

The raid of 1820 and the court case of the Voudou Virgin in 1850 provide crucial documentation of a likely representation of Mami Wata in the context of Voudou during that time in New Orleans. It is strong evidence that links New Orleans Voudou to West Africa; yet, the African link to New Orleans Voudou is often doubted and discredited by scholars. Some have even suggested there is no link to Africa and that New Orleans Voudou is derived from Haitian Vodou. This is patently incorrect. While there is no doubt that elements of Haitian Vodou can be found in New Orleans Voudou, the African link is stronger. Africa is the well from which the Voudou spring was sprung in Louisiana.

Papa Labas and St. Peter

Meanwhile, we get another small clue to another African spirit connected to Marie Laveau's Voudou practice in one of the Louisiana Writers' Project interviews of an ex-enslaved woman named Josephine McDuffy, born in 1853. She recounts hearing passersby on their way to a St. John's Eve celebration and she tells her husband she wants to go join them. Despite his objections, she goes anyway. Along the way she meets up with a white woman from the neighborhood who asks her where she is going. "I'm going to see Marie Laveau," Josephine says. "I'm going to see Papa Limba . . . Papa Limba [Labas] is supposed to be St. Peter" (Dillon 1940). This little reference tells us that syncretism was still functioning at that time as a cover for the African gods. Papa Limba, or Labas, is who we refer to as Papa Legba today; and St. Peter is the Catholic saint syncretized with him. Papa Legba is the gatekeeper to the spirit world and is represented by keys, among other things, while St. Peter holds the keys to the gates of heaven. Beyond this similarity, however, the two have little in common.

In New Orleans Voudou, syncretism manifests as Catholic icons representing African deities. The introduction of Catholic saints is a direct result of the implementation of the Louisiana Black Code, which made the practice of any religion other than Catholicism illegal. Substituting images of Catholic saints that shared similar characteristics as the Voudou spirits allowed slaves to continue with their religions in a veiled manner. Over time, the saints became incorporated into New Orleans Voudou as separate entities unto themselves, not substitutions. In Louisiana, it was easy to blend Voudou and Catholicism because of the many similarities between the two traditions. Both believe in a Supreme Being along with lesser beings that act as intermediaries between people and God. Both include symbolic or actual rituals of sacrifice, and both use altars as focal points of devotion.

St. Maroon

As mentioned in the earlier section Slave Owner, the description given of Marie Laveau's altar indicated she had a statue of St. Maroon. We can assume from this report that St. Maroon was a part of her spiritual court. St. Maroon is known among modern-day devotees as one of her favorite saints. Again, some people express confusion or doubt about the identity of St. Maroon, but in New Orleans Voudou and Laveau Voudou, such doubt does not exist. St. Maroon refers to Jean Saint Malo, aka Juan San Malò, a leader of a large system of Maroon colonies in the cypress swamps surrounding colonial New Orleans in the 1700s. The territory controlled by St. Maroon is referred to as Ville Gaillarde and was comprised of the southeastern area between New Orleans and the eastern shore of Lake Borgne (Hall 1992, 212). He and his fellow Africans carved out niche communities in the swamps for runaway slaves with the help of local Native Americans. Jean Saint Malo is said to have buried his hatchet in the first cypress tree of Gaillard Island, saying, *"Malheur au blanc qui passera ces bornes,"* meaning, "Woe to the white who would pass this boundary" (Hall 1992, 213). The boundary was the Louisiana swamps.

Jean Saint Malo was ultimately executed on June 19, 1784, in front of the St. Louis Cathedral. He was denied a proper burial; instead, his body was left hanging to rot for days while his bones were picked and collected as treasured gris gris by practitioners. After his death, he was elevated quickly to sainthood due to his incredible deeds. The spirit of Jean Saint Malo was subsequently sought out by Voudouists and runaway slaves alike to provide protection and safe passage for slaves seeking freedom.

As slavery became a thing of the past, St. Maroon has become a more obscure saint and tends to stay on the altars of those old-school Voudous practicing on the down low. Some local New Orleans Voudou practitioners, such as the Divine Prince Ty Emmecca, however, have performed public rituals and poured libations in the French Quarter in his honor on his feast day. It would seem that we could use St. Maroon's assistance when reparations are on the table and folks are embracing their heritage and reclaiming their historical narratives. He is still available and accessible to practitioners and devotees who may seek assistance for today's emergent crisis of immigrants seeking asylum in this country, as well as those seeking to connect with ancestral spirits. St. Maroon's feast day is June 19.

Yon Sue and St. Anthony

Marie Laveau is said to have favored St. Anthony of Padua, who may be petitioned either as the Catholic saint or as the African spirit with whom he is syncretized, Yon Sue or Monsieur Agassou. St. Anthony also happens to be the patron saint of the Kongo. Tallant, Pitkin, and Ellis all report that Saint Anthony is petitioned as Yon Sue or Monsieur Agassou; he is also associated with Papa Legba by some folks. Yon Sue is said to manifest as a great guardian who protects Voudouists from those who would interfere with their freedom to worship the spirits of Africa. Represented as a leopard, he is kept alongside statues of St. Anthony with a red ribbon tied around him. He is petitioned for protection and for money.

According to oral tradition, Marie kept a statue of St. Anthony by the front door. When she was busy with a client or doing conjure work, she would turn the statue on his head. When folks came by to seek her help and advice, they knew to wait until she turned him right side up before knocking on the door.

Part Two

BECOMING
A
DEVOTEE

Figure 11. A tabletop altar to Marie Laveau with Li Grand Zombi and Elegba fetishes, a Marie Laveau doll, and a Mother lodestone. *Courtesy of author*

Developing a Respectful Servitude

•••

She had wonderful knowledge of the toxic properties of herbs and roots and no less marvelous skill in extracting and compounding these poisons. For gain or revenge, for black or white, she was always ready to use her skill and was feared by every negro in the city and surrounding country as a dealer in black art.

—*RICHMOND DAILY PALLADIUM,* 1900.

Most modern-day Marie Laveau devotees believe in Jesus and the saints, just as Madame Marie did. They go to church, pray the rosary, and work the gris gris. They volunteer in the community, feed folks when they are hungry, and are always ready to assist someone in need. Of course, each devotee aspires to honor Marie Laveau in their own way, in the best way they can. They know her values and they know her style. Increasingly, there are people who are devotees who are not Catholic or churchgoers but embrace a charitable lifestyle in ways that are meaningful to them.

It's a powerful thing to witness someone doing Madame Marie's work. When it's real, there's no denying it. It is something that can be felt within the core of your being. Devotees have presence. When you become a devotee—when you are aware of your spiritual lineage, learn about it, and live it—then you can fully embrace your new identity and Marie Laveau, the loa, spirit guide, and elevated Ancestor—can descend and work through you.

Devoting yourself to someone or something requires a conscious decision to do so followed by deliberate actions that display your utmost loyalty to the focus of your devotion. Becoming a devotee is not a decision to be made lightly. It can change your life for better or worse, depending on the sincerity of your commitment. If you are ready and you are open to receiving her as the Mother of New Orleans Voudou, the Spiritual Mother of Louisiana, the Boss Woman and Queen, your life will change dramatically for the better because of how you will be required to live your life. You must be ready to put others' needs before your own in order to reap the benefits of personal gain. There's nothing wrong with wanting a better life and material things, but there is always an energetic give-and-take with all manifestations. If you live the kind of life Marie Laveau lived, you will automatically deposit goodness into the Bank of Karma instead of the opposite, and, well, it just makes good cosmic sense.

On the other hand, if you are looking for a spirit you can "use" to get back your man or influence a court decision by simply lighting a candle and uttering a few words of intent, then becoming a devotee of Marie Laveau is probably not the path for you. Think of it this way: If you had a direct line to the Queen of England, would you call her up and ask her to buy you dinner for a month? Followed up with a, "Let it be so"? Probably not. You have to think of your relationship with Madame Marie as if she were a living, breathing human being and base your interactions on courtesy and common sense. Becoming a devotee is a commitment, it is a journey, and it takes time to learn and to develop a relationship with not only Marie Laveau but all those in her spiritual court with whom you will want to share blessings.

In Creole Voodoo, Marie Laveau is recognized as an elevated Ancestor. Some refer to her as a saint. In Voodoo terms, she is a loa. She is not merely a spirit guide, as some purport her to be, although she is that as well. She smiles favorably upon those who know how to serve her correctly. She is kind and gentle and wise, but I have also seen her as a stern mother who is not afraid to literally smack someone upside the head for disrespecting her (recall Elmore Lee Banks's story). Once, there was a guy who thought it was a good idea to leave a dead water moccasin at the foot of her tomb as an offering. On his way home, he got into an accident and ended up with a broken leg. I'm not saying she did it, but I'm not saying she didn't, either. Maybe he was distracted, or maybe he was a terrible driver. Maybe it wasn't his fault, and someone hit him. Maybe it was instant karma. Who knows? (By the way, a dead snake is the worst thing anyone could ever leave as an offering, considering Voudou's primary deity is Damballah Wedo, the sacred serpent. That would be like leaving a dead Jesus at the tomb of the Pope.) Marie Laveau is a strong female spirit who knows her worth and commands respect in spirit as well as in life. To be a devotee, you must be informed or face the consequences of your choice to be ignorant and dismissive.

This is why I have spent a good part of this book talking about who Marie Laveau was as a woman and about the challenges she faced in society. New Orleans is a wonderful city, but let's face it—she has a dark side and a dark history. She's been thrown out of balance. Hell, I don't know if she has ever been in balance, truth be told. Maybe this is one reason gris gris was one of those traditions that survived the creolization process, because it serves as a mechanism for restoring balance. And it is ultra flexible in form; its reach goes from charm to weapon of war. Some folks say gris gris means "grey grey" in French, referring to magick in the middle ground—not black, not white, but a more realistic approach to magick; one that parallels real life. This explanation is a local one and not based on its history as an Islamic tradition, but I believe it has some merit nonetheless. After all, traditions change in a malleable culture, as people adapt them to suit their needs in ways that carry the most function and meaning. We will delve more into gris gris later in the book.

THE LAVEAU LEGITIMACY FACTOR

This has always been a common practice, to assume the name of a well-known predecessor.

HARRY MIDDLETON HYATT, 1970

Identifying as a spiritual worker in the Marie Laveau tradition provides a certain degree of legitimacy and power for conjure workers, both past and present. Many conjure workers of old claimed association with her to boost public perception of their power and effectiveness. In a newspaper article written in *The Kimball Graphic* in 1886, for example, one such worker by the name of Dr. Clapion[5] was summoned by a family member of a man who was believed to have been hoodooed. Dr. Clapion describes his ancestry and powers thus:

> I was the son-in-law of Marie Leveau, queen of the voudoos, who died several years ago. I learned at her house to exercise the power of the gift I had received, and since then I have studied the art. I never do harm to anyone, nor do I charge a cent for my services. When I am called, I go and do not ask for recompense. My trade is that of house and sign painting, but if my services to heal the sick or accomplish some good act are needed, I am always ready. I do not profess medicine as a calling.

Notable folklorist and anthropologist Zora Neale Hurston reported on her encounters with conjure doctors in New Orleans claiming kinship with Marie Laveau as well. She describes one of the conjure doctors who initiated her thus: "Anatole Pierre, of New Orleans, was a middle-aged octoroon. He is a Catholic and lays some feeble claim to kinship with Marie Laveau" (Hurston 1935, 207). Another of her teachers, Luke Turner, claimed to be Marie Laveau's nephew and even expounded on his relationship with her, but not in a way that proves actual kinship. He describes seeing her emerge from Lake Pontchartrain during a feast where the celebrants called upon her:

> She would rise out of the waters of the lake with a great communion candle burning on her head and another in each one of her hands. She walked upon the waters to the shore. As a little boy, I saw her myself. When the feast was over, she went back into the lake, and nobody saw her for nine days again.
>
> On the feast that I saw her open the waters, she looked hard at me and nodded her head so that her tignon shook. Then I knew I was called to take up her work. She was very old, and I was a lad

of seventeen. Soon I went to wait on her altar, both at her house on St. Ann Street and her house on Bayou St. John's (Hurston 1935, 193–194).

As in the past, modern conjurers and Spiritualists frequently take on the Laveau name in the belief that it will add "street cred" to their reputations and give them an upper hand with their competitors. As far as I am aware, none of these modern-day "faux Laveaus" actually descended from the Voodoo Queen, however, and many are not even from New Orleans. Marie Laveau and her magick have been commercialized, appropriated, and subjected to frauds and cons by those who do not understand or appreciate the magnitude of contributions she made to New Orleans culture and history. She solidified a magicospiritual tradition spearheaded mostly by women that had been in a state of flux since the first enslaved West Africans set foot in Louisiana. From her, New Orleans Voudou as a folk religion emerged. From her entrepreneurial spirit, the business of Hoodoo became a thing. For these achievements, the New Orleans tourist trade—as well as everyone using her name in a business capacity—has much to be grateful for.

WALKING THE PATH

There are many ways to live a life of devotion in the path of Marie Laveau. Find your skills, your creativity, and your passion, and volunteer in ways that show it. Being a volunteer rosary maker is one way I do this. Every rosary made is an act of devotion consistent with her legacy. It is something I can do as someone with a chronic illness where committing to going to the soup kitchen or something similar isn't an option. I can make these from my bed when I'm not feeling well or wherever when I'm feeling good. It doesn't cost me anything but time, as the club sends the supplies to its members.

Another way of being charitable is to add that dollar to your pizza or grocery purchase for sick kids. But one of my favorite ways to walk the talk is to create bags of helpful necessities to give to homeless people: canned food (be sure to choose cans that don't require a can opener; otherwise, include a can opener), water, toilet paper, soap, socks, wipes, a list of local services, a handwritten affirmation . . . you get the idea. Make bags for women, with feminine hygiene products and lip gloss. Also, prepare some bags with dog food and a sweater for folks with dogs. Prepare them in advance to keep in your car, so that you may give when you see someone in need.

Another way to be charitable that I really love is to be a secret conjure saint. This is great for folks with a little extra cash to spare and is a variation of the popular Blessed Bucks Spell that was apparently started in 1989 by a Wiccan woman who went by the internet screen name Tiger Lilly[6]. The idea is to bless some money by writing the following on each bill: "May you be blessed with health, wealth, and joy." Then secretly leave the money where others will find it. According to the Wiccan Rule of Three, everything you do comes back to you threefold, so when you do this, it is said you will be blessed in triplicate.

My version of blessed money is more in alignment with the Marie Laveau path of devotion. Take some dollar bills in whatever denomination you can afford and wash them in a mild solution of soap and water to which a dash of Florida Water or Hoyt's Cologne has been added. Lay them out to dry and iron flat. Then, anoint each of the four corners in addition to the center of the dollar bill with Abundance Oil (petitions may be fixed this way as well). This is called *fixing* your money. You may write a blessing on the dollar bill, if you wish. Now, take the bills and leave them in places where people will likely find them. For example, tape one to a package of diapers, insert one in a new purse or wallet, stick one in a coat pocket, or place one in a book. Hiding the money must be a covert activity, so be sure that no one sees what you are doing. What you are doing here is giving blessings without attachment. From this act of generosity comes a rush of adrenaline and dopamine, as you feel the joy in giving with no expectations. Imagine people's reactions when they find one! Another wonderful side effect of this activity is that you will often find you are blessed in return in ways you would never expect. This, of course, is the Law of Attraction at work, where everything you do attracts like energy.

If you don't have much money, you can still be a secret conjure saint using pennies. Everyone has a few pennies lying around. Gather as many pennies as you can and wash them in a mild soap solution and then rinse in saltwater or Florida Water to cleanse them. I am partial to Hoyt's Cologne for this, but as it is increasingly harder to find, it may not be an option for you unless you make some yourself. In any event, prepare your pennies and as you are washing and rinsing, pray Psalm 23. Lay them out to dry, and when dried, add to a green flannel mojo bag along with a piece of pyrite and High John the Conqueror root. Then, pray one of the following psalms over the pennies (just choose one that matches the blessings you would like the ultimate penny possessors to be gifted):

- For quick money and good health, read Psalm 81

- To attract money, happiness, and success, read Psalms 54 and 71

- To attract money and work, read Psalm 61

- To bring money, luck, and financial success, read Psalm 150 three times

Once your pennies are cleansed, dressed, and blessed, carry them with you when you go out and strategically toss a few on the ground where you know people will be walking and likely pick them up for "good luck." Little will they know just how lucky that penny is!

Another thing you can do to uplift others is to place magickal affirmations in random places. But you have to fix the paper onto which they will be written first. The ritual of the preparation sets your intention. Any kind of paper will work—from the fanciest of papers to an ordinary brown paper sack. Cut or tear your paper into strips—the size doesn't really matter. Your writing implement could be anything from a special feather dipped in an inkwell to a simple black pen or fine-point marker. If using an inkwell, use Dove's Blood Ink (for love, reconciliation, and affection) or Dragon's Blood Ink (for protection, defense, power, and courage). Write any heartfelt message you wish to impart upon the world. Affirmations are written in first person present tense, as if they are already manifest. Follow by "So be it," so when the person reads it, they are actually uttering an incantation which activates the affirmation into fruition. Here are a few examples:

I am held in the sacred embrace of the Divine. So be it.

Relief from struggle is here. So be it.

I am a sacred and divine human being. So be it.

All is a blessing. So be it.

My guardian angel is watching over me. So be it.

Magickal affirmations can be left in random places like public bathrooms, on restaurant tables or seats, even in your child's lunchbox!

Barring any of the above ideas, there are a multitude of ways you can serve your community. Volunteer at a local animal shelter. Volunteer to rock babies at a local hospital. Volunteer at your local community garden or start one if there isn't one in your neighborhood. Crochet blankets for the needy. Help out your local veterans. If you are a professional, offer pro bono services on occasion. Check out the classifieds, and ask around to see where you might fit in. There is a place for everyone. If you can't find something, you either aren't looking hard enough or want the easy way out. Woe is you should the latter be your motivation.

These are just a few ideas you can implement to live as a Marie Laveau devotee. Consciously incorporate random acts of kindness in your life whenever the opportunity presents itself. Pay things forward in honor of Marie Laveau. Humanity and charity must come first; magick is second. The magick does not matter if you don't do charity work of some sort when following the path of a Marie Laveau devotee. Once charity is a natural part of your life, the magick you perform in her name will be unparalleled.

Now you have an idea of what it means to become a devotee of Marie Laveau. If you are not sure this is the path for you, simply read the information and think about it. There is always time to serve her should you decide you want to give it a try. If and when you are ready, the next step is creating an altar for her so that you can begin developing a regular devotional service to her.

Figure 12. A working New Orleans Voudou altar to Marie Laveau.
Courtesy of author

Creating an Altar
of Devotion

•••

Voudou altars consist of a number of common elements no matter the spirit or saint called upon and served. These common elements are not seen in traditional African altar spaces and most likely derive from Catholicism. As Laveau Voudou is influenced by Catholicism in addition to African traditions, we observe these commonalities when creating altars for Marie Laveau. The use of white altar cloths and the presence of flowers, candles, a cross, and incense, for example, are all described as required altar items in the *General Instruction of the Roman Missal.* Strict adherence to the most elaborate and decorated altar space is not required, however, as there are many variations on a theme. Our Voudou Queen will appreciate any sincere effort to show reverence.

One issue that will determine the type and complexity of altar space you create is your budget. For some people this is not an issue and they can afford the best offerings at all times. This is not the case for most folks. Maintaining an altar with fresh flowers can be costly, for example, but even the Church allows for substitutions in the form of "good-quality artificial ones" (Schulte), and Marie used artificial flowers when creating altars for inmates. So, if you are strapped for cash, invest in some high-quality artificial flowers to be kept on her altar and supplement with fresh ones when you can. I like to spray artificial flowers with perfume when freshening up her altar and when working with her. But remember, even a single fresh flower will be appreciated when you can afford it. Also, gathering wildflowers as they come into bloom is a fantastic, economical alternative

Table 1. Marie Laveau Characteristics

Born	Marie Catherine Laveaux
	September 10, 1801 French Quarter, New Orleans, Louisiana
Died	June 15, 1881 (age 79) New Orleans, Louisiana
Resting Place	St. Louis Cemetery No. 1
Nationality	Afro-Creole American
Occupation	Beautician, Nurse, Voodoo Queen
Spouses	Jacques Paris, Christophe Glapion
Feast Days	June 15 (Marie's death); June 23–24, St. John the Baptist Day (the most important holiday in New Orleans Voudou); September 10 (Marie's birthday)
Venerated in	New Orleans Voudou
Attributes	White tignon tied in seven knots like a crown, shawl, snake, rooster, feather, gris gris bag, and gold hoop earrings
Colors	Blue, white
Offerings	Fresh flowers; healing-related items like a mortar and pestle, herbs, and roots; beauty-related items like mirrors, combs, and head scarves; gris gris; images of saints; rosaries; chaplets; money; voodoo dolls; incense; perfumes; silver and gold jewelry; alligator heads; Hoodoo curios; magickal oils and powders; saltwater; a photo of her tomb in a nice frame; blue and white candles; New Orleans–themed items, such as beads, doubloons, and Mardi Gras keepsakes. The best offering is to donate to the poor and volunteer in her name to help those who are less fortunate.
Food Offerings	Hoppin' John, congris, money greens, gumbo, jambalaya, sweets, French pastries, pumpkins, sweet potatoes, coffee and chicory, white rum, French wine, champagne, anisette, candy, cornbread, hoe cakes, French bread, seafood, all Creole foods and soul foods
Number	7
Patronage	Rootworkers, herbalists, healers, nurses, beauticians, New Orleans, New Orleans Voudouists, runaway slaves, orphans, market women, Catholic mystics
Petition for	Love, court cases, business success, family harmony, justice, empowerment, all life conditions, to empower any working
Ritual Symbol	

to buying costly flowers from florists that have often lost their fragrance. I do this all the time and almost always have seasonal wildflowers and blooms from trees and bushes that adorn her altar.

Generally, there are three types of traditional altars to Marie Laveau: the parterre, the three-tiered altar, and the tabletop altar. Three-tiered altars are often reserved for saints, such as the elaborate St. Joseph altars found all around New Orleans on St. Joseph's Day and Mardi Gras. Tabletop altars are consistent with conjure workers. Parterres are used in both Voodoo and Hoodoo. The type of altar you choose to build for Marie Laveau will depend on your available space and resources. By no means does this mean she won't appreciate any sacred space you make for her. I have made large, three-tiered altars to her that take up an entire wall, as well as simple tabletop altars. I have even only had her image hanging on the wall and also made portable shrines to her from Altoids tins when space was an issue.

As you work with Marie Laveau, remember that she is best served with her favorite things and colors. Keep the guidelines from Table 1 handy when working with her, creating her altar, and giving her offerings. There is a lot of room for personalization, so consider the information in the table on page 80 as a guideline.

THE PARTERRE

A parterre is an arrangement of offerings spread out on the ground on a white cloth. The color white is used because it is associated with the Ancestors in African-derived traditions. In African and Western cultures, white is a symbol of purity and cleanliness. In the context of Catholicism, the *General Instruction of the Roman Missal* states: "Out of reverence for the celebration of the memorial of the Lord and for the banquet in which the Body and Blood of the Lord are offered, there should be, on an altar where this is celebrated, at least one cloth, white in colour, whose shape, size, and decoration are in keeping with the altar's structure." In addition, Catholic regulations of the nineteenth and early twentieth century stipulate that

Figure 13. A Voodoo dance from *Century Illustrated Magazine*, 1885–1886. This drawing illustrates the parterre used in Voudou rituals characteristic of the 1800s.

altar cloths be made of linen or hemp as opposed to any other material, even if of a higher quality. Of course, folks nowadays will use any sort of white cloth without understanding the origins behind the practice.

Parterres can be indoors or outdoors. They have candles burning in the four corners of the cloth and/or the room, and the color of the candles signifies the purpose of the gathering (e.g., green for money, white for blessings, red for love or power). An image of a saint may be placed in the center of the layout if a saint is invoked for the working. A good example of a parterre from the early part of the twentieth century is described in an article by a writer for the Louisiana Works Progress Administration (WPA). The article, entitled "Description of a Hoodoo Opening Ceremony to Make a Person a Member of the Sect," is an account of an initiation ritual undergone by the writer. A worker called Nom "made an altar on the floor with a white cloth (it was clean and pressed, about the size of an average tablecloth)" and placed an image of St. Peter in the center of the cloth, noting St. Peter was used because he "opens the gates of heaven." The writer goes on to describe the offerings that were placed on the cloth and how they were arranged:

Green and white candles were lit on the cloth, rather, slightly off of the cloth; other candles were placed around the picture. Nom placed two quart size bottles on the altar, one of cider and the other of raspberry pop. Several plates were put on the altar. In one plate was some steel dust which was on the right side of the picture, orris root powder was placed in front of the picture, a plate of dry basile was in the center of the picture and to the front near the center was a plate of stage planks (cake) and a box of ginger snaps. To the left of the cakes was a plate of mixed bird seed. To the rear of this was a plate of cloves; to the right was cinnamon. On each side of this were the pans of con-gris, which was cooked red beans and rice. A small bottle of olive oil was to the left of the picture with a bag of sugar to the left of this, slightly off the cloth or altar. There was a bunch of bananas on the left side and some apples on the right. After arranging the powders etc. Nom placed a piece of camphor branch near the picture, also a glass of bastille. The camphor represented a palm. A half-pint of gin was placed in the center front while a bottle of Jax beer was put to the left of the picture (McKinney n.d.)

It should be noted that the camphor branch is associated with opening roads and would have been a fitting amplification of St. Peter's role in the ritual. Whether or not it was actually a substitution for a palm branch is not known; however, palm branches are not hard to find in Louisiana, so it is a bit of a conundrum as to why "camphor represented a palm."

Another description of a Voudou parterre was observed by a couple of reporters for the *Times Democrat* in 1884. The reporters heard about a Voudou dance that was supposed to occur one evening and set out to find it. What they stumbled upon was the revival of the celebration of St. John's Eve by a Voudou queen and her attendants. By invitation, they gained entrance to the ceremony so long as they agreed to abide by the rules, lest the charm would not work. They described seeing several people sitting on the ground around the edges of the room, and in the center of the room was a white tablecloth on the ground with tallow candles stuck to each corner of the cloth in their own wax:

> As a centre-piece, on the cloth, there was a shallow Indian basket filled with weeds or, as they called them, herbes. Around the basket were diminutive piles of white beans and corn, and just outside of these a number of small bones, whether human or not could not be told. Some curiously wrought bunches of feathers were the next ornamentations near the edge of the cloth, and outside of all several saucers with small cakes in them.

The reporters inquired as to the identity of the Voudou Queen, and they were told it was Malvina Latour. She was dressed in a blue calico dress and "on her head a brilliant tignon was gracefully tied." Latour was noted as the only one in the room "enjoying the aristocratic privilege of a chair" (*Times Democrat* 1884).

To create a parterre-style altar for Marie Laveau, start by laying out a clean white tablecloth on the ground. On each corner, set a white candle. In the center, set an image of the Voudou Queen. Place one blue candle in front of her image and a white candle on either side of the center blue candle. In front of the blue candle, set a clear glass of water with a crucifix laid on top, congris, and a variety of her other favorite offerings, using the table of Marie Laveau characteristics as a guide. Lay a single red rose near her photo. Personalize the altar in a manner that speaks to you. Light some incense. Perfumes and pleasant fragrances are effective means of drawing spirits down when you need their attention. Your altar is now ready for your petition, prayer, or meditation. Light your candles and incense, knock three times on the ground, and call out Marie Laveau's name three times. Then proceed with your service or petition.

THREE-TIERED ALTAR

The most common style of traditional altar for Marie Laveau among Voudouists, particularly for her feast day, is the three-tiered altar. This may be in part due to her partiality to creating these types of altars herself as seen in the earlier section, Prison Ministry and Court Work. However, it is likely Marie was influenced by the Church for creating this style of altar. To set up a three-tiered altar, you will need the following items:

- Table (bottom tier)

- 2 elevations for subsequent tiers—these could be sturdy boxes, shelves, even stacks of books (one should be larger than the other)

- Blue and white cloth

- An image of her tomb, framed

- 2 bunches of flowers

- Blue or white vases

- 7 white glass-encased candles

- Pretty cobalt blue or white plate

- Beautician-related items such as mirrors, combs, brushes, perfumes, hairsprays, hair ribbons, and the like

- New Orleans–themed items such as Mardi Gras beads, doubloons (especially with her image), Voodoo dolls

- Healing-related items such as a mortar and pestle, thermometer, roots, herbs, and medicines

- Statues or framed images of Papa Legba, Ellegua, St. Anthony, St. Peter, St. Expedite, St. Joseph, Mother Mary, and/or St. Jude

- Your best found gris gris

- Clear glass of water

- Crucifix

- A wooden box for your gris gris

- Image or doll of Marie Laveau

- Snake figurine—king snake, water moccasin, rattlesnake, python, or boa constrictor (the python and boa constrictor represent Li Grand Zombi; the others represent her signature snake conjure—they are two separate things and are NOT interchangeable)

- 1 special blue candle

- Rosary or chaplet

First Tier

This is the bottom tier. Drape a blue cloth over a table or lay it on the ground. On the center front, place the framed image of Marie's tomb. On either side of the cloth, place fresh flowers in blue or white vases. Place four candles at the four cardinal points of the lower tier. Place your various offerings on this level. The arrangement is not as important as its aesthetic appeal (remember, she likes pretty—queenly pretty). Place a cobalt blue or white plate for her food offerings on this level.

Figure 14. Three-tiered altar to Marie Laveau. *Courtesy of Amy Hedrick*

Second Tier

Place the elevation shelf on top center toward the back. Drape this layer with another blue or white cloth. On either side, place images of St. Anthony and St. Peter (you can substitute Legba for St. Peter). Place three more white candles—two on either side, and one in the middle. You can place more flowers on both sides of this level. Add a clear glass of water with a crucifix laid across the top. In the center front, place your gris gris box. Keep any gris gris you make to charge up in this box for seven days for full consecration.

Third Tier

Place the third elevated shelf on top center and drape with another blue cloth. Place an image of Marie Laveau in the middle of the top layer, with a snake figurine at her feet and the special blue candle next to her but not in front of her. Keep her chaplet on this level.

The reason for the three separate cloths is to prevent slippage, which can happen with one larger cloth draping over all three tiers.

TABLETOP ALTAR

The tabletop altar is the most common type used by people who come into the tradition from outside of New Orleans. To make a tabletop altar, simply arrange the items listed above on a table or dresser top. Important items to include would be a focal object representing her in the center, surrounded by images of saints (at least Mother Mary and St. Anthony), two white candles, one blue candle, a clear glass of water with a crucifix, and other items listed you may have on hand. Don't forget the wall space behind the altar where you can hang images of Marie Laveau or her saints, or her ritual symbol, referred to as a vévé.

Figure 15. This image of the painting of Marie Laveau by Frank Schneider is likely the same one the Voudou Queen La La cut out and framed and put on her altar. Credit: Hammond, Hilda Phelps. 1930. "Behind the Veil of Voodooism in America." Dayton Daily News, 5 Oct. 1930 *(www.newspapers.com)*

Petitioning Marie Laveau

•••

Once you have Marie Laveau's altar set up, you need to spend some time developing a relationship with her. The first order of business is to formally introduce yourself by name, so she knows who you are. Tell her a little about yourself. Think of how you would address an elder you meet for the first time. Talk to her daily. Light a single white or blue candle for her. Do not ask her for anything for at least the first month. Simply light a candle, pray for her, for her children, and for the healing of the women in her family. Mambo Sallie Ann Glassman suggests the following litany can be said during any invocation or petitioning of the Voodoo Queen:

> For Marie Laveau, historical lwa of New Orleans. Vodou Queen. Strong, intelligent, wise and powerful woman. During your life you danced with the Invisibles, and in death you dance with us. Accept our offerings. Enter into our hearts, our arms, our legs. Enter and dance with us! (Glassman 2000, 53)

Following is a prayer that I wrote for Marie years ago. Feel free to say the prayer to her on a daily basis as you develop a relationship with her.

PRAYER TO MARIE LAVEAU

Holy Mother of New Orleans Voudou, hear my prayer.

I humbly request your assistance.

Through you I feel the gentle power of Divine Justice.

Give me strength to stand against my enemies and protect me from
*   those who wish me harm,*

Sweet Heart of Marie, Show me your wisdom

That I shall speak the truth and elevate the Ancestors

Madame Marie, Bless me with the protection of Johnny Conker

That he shall always have my back.

Holy Mother of New Orleans Voudou, Bless me with the powers of the Sacred Serpent Li Grand Zombi

That I may walk in balance, equally male and female.

Holy Mother of New Orleans Voudou, Bless me with the spirit of St. Maroon

That I shall never take for granted the freedoms that I have.

And with the light that emanates from your Spirit, Madame Laveaux, all darkness is Obsolete.

Holy Mother of New Orleans Voudou, pray for me.

Holy Mother of New Orleans Voudou, hear my plea.

Holy Mother of New Orleans Voudou, Madame Marie, pray for me.

Ashe!

Whenever you petition Marie Laveau for a favor of any kind, you will need to provide her with some offerings (refer to Table 1 on page 80). Place the offerings on her altar on the bottom tier and say to her, "Madame Laveau, do you see these offering I have given you? You are the most powerful and most beautiful of all the Voodoo queens. Come and partake of these gifts I have for you!" Then, ask her for what you need. Be sure to thank her when all is said and done. Honor Madame Laveau by making a charitable donation in her name or doing a random act of kindness.

ASKING MARIE LAVEAU TO EMPOWER YOUR WORK

One way to work with Marie Laveau is to ask her to empower your conjure at the time you are doing a working. This tip comes from another Voudou Queen in New Orleans, Laura Hopkins, also known as La La. A Voudou Queen in New Orleans during the 1930s and 1940s, La La attributed her conjure style to Marie Laveau. She stated that she used to go to Marie Laveau's home on St. Ann Street and peer in the windows and watch her work. She also stated that Marie taught her. La La kept a small altar in the corner of her room with Marie Laveau's picture in it that she had cut out of the newspaper (see figure 15). La La shared in an interview with the Louisiana Writers' Project that after she prepares her working, she sets it before the image of Marie Laveau. She then says a short prayer: "Marie, yo' da greatest—yo' help me do my work" (Wallace 1940, 3).

La La is quite the character, and I would have loved to have met her. She had a notorious reputation, described by locals as "a devil, she wears a shawl over her head to hide her horns," and "dere ain't no tellin' what dat woman will do to yo', she's jes wicked" (Wallace 1940, 1). When interviewed, she seemed to be hiding out from the locals in the neighborhood and was concerned about the interviewer being the police. She described herself as working with both hands, meaning she worked harms and cures. "Sho, I do good—I has to laff 'cause I do more wicked" (Wallace 1940, 5). La La was a shameless self-promoter, telling the interviewer how good she was and everything she accomplished for people. Yet, she never said she was as good as or better than Marie Laveau: "I'm good, but not like Marie Laveau. She's a crack" (Wallace 1940, 4).

Follow in La La's footsteps when doing works for yourself or others and always ask Marie Laveau to bless your work beforehand. Like La La, it is best to ask in your own words so that it is heartfelt and comes from you rather than a recitation of a phrase someone else writes.

THE MARIE LAVEAU CHAPLET

The term *chaplet* is used to designate Roman Catholic prayer forms that use prayer beads but are not necessarily related to the rosary. Chaplets are associated with Jesus, Mary, and the saints. Chaplets are considered personal devotionals—they have no set form, and therefore they vary considerably. While the usual five-decade rosary may be referred to as a chaplet, chaplets often have fewer beads than a traditional rosary and a different set of prayers.

The chaplet of Marie Laveau is composed of nine beads, a crucifix, and a Marie Laveau medal. It begins with the crucifix, and three sets of three beads. The last set of three beads is composed of two stones and one glass bead. Say the chaplet of Marie Laveau daily to develop a relationship with her.

Figure 16. Marie Laveau chaplet by the author.

Start the chaplet on the crucifix by making the sign of the cross, holding the chaplet in your right hand:

In the name of the Father (touch your right hand to your forehead),

and of the Son (move your right hand to touch your heart),

and of the Holy Spirit (move your right hand to your left shoulder and then to your right shoulder),

Amen (kiss the crucifix and fold your hands over your heart).

On the first set of three beads, say:

Sweet Heart of Marie, be my inspiration.

Then say the Prayer to the Holy Spirit by St. Augustine.

PRAYER TO THE HOLY SPIRIT

Breathe into me, Holy Spirit,

that my thoughts may all be holy.

Move in me, Holy Spirit,

that my work, too, may be holy.

Attract my heart, Holy Spirit,

that I may love only what is holy.

Strengthen me, Holy Spirit,

that I may defend all that is holy.

Protect me, Holy Spirit,

that I may always be holy.

On the second set of three beads, say the Litany of Marie Laveau.

LITANY OF MARIE LAVEAU

Holy Mother, the Lwas and Orishas, the Saints, the Angels, the Ancestors, and the Dead

Holy Mother Marie, I honor you and all the Lwas and Orishas: Dr. John, Papa Legba, Ellegua, Exu, Pomba Gira, Oya, Oshun, Obàtálá, Ogun, Yemaya, la Sirene, La Baleine, Chango, John the Conqueror, Erzulie Dantor, Erzulie Freda, Annie Christmas, Damballah, Ayida Wedo, the Marassa, Blanc Dani, Mait Carrefour, Mami Wata, Li Grand Zombi, and all other Lwas and Orishas. And I pray, Sweet Heart of Marie, be my strength.

Holy Mother Marie, I honor you and all the Saints of New Orleans: St. John the Baptist, St. Anne, St. Joseph, St. Roch, St. Jude, St. Anthony, St. Maroon, St. Expedite, Black Hawk, St. Michael the Archangel, Queen Esther, Our Lady of Mercy, Our Lady of Guadalupe, St. Barbara, St. Benedict, Our Lady of Prompt Succor, Our Lady of Perpetual Help, St. Frances, St. Patrick, St. Peter, St. Mary Magdalene, and all other saints. And I pray, Sweet Heart of Marie, be my strength.

Holy Mother Marie, I honor you and all the heavenly Spirits and Angels: all the seraphim, cherubim, powers, and dominations, all the sovereignties, all the archangels, all the guardian angels, and my guardian angel. And I pray, Sweet Heart of Marie, be my strength.

To the spirits of the living and the spirits of the Dead, the Ancestors, les Morts, the Guédé, the Barons, Manman Brigit, Papa Guédé, Oya, and all others. And I pray, Sweet Heart of Marie, be my strength.

On the third set of three beads, say the following on each bead:

Sweet Heart of Marie, grant me thy wisdom.

Then say the Prayer to the Seven African Powers on the first two beads. On the third special bead, pray from your heart for your need and state your petition.

PRAYER TO THE SEVEN AFRICAN POWERS

Oh, Seven African Powers, who are so

close to our Divine Savior, with great humility

I kneel before thee and implore your intercession.

My heart tells me that my petition is righteous.

If you were to grant it, I would add even more glory to the holy name of
God our Father.

Amen.

On the Marie Laveau medal, say:

Holy Mother of New Orleans Voudou, hear my prayer.

I humbly request your assistance.

Through you I feel the gentle power of Divine Justice.

Give me strength to stand against my enemies

and protect me from those who wish me harm,

Sweet Heart of Marie, Show me your wisdom

That I shall speak the truth and elevate the Ancestors

Queen Marie, Bless me with the protection of Johnny Conker

That he shall always have my back.

Holy Mother of New Orleans Voudou,

Bless me with the powers of the Sacred Serpents Li Grand Zombi,
Damballah, and Ayida Wedo,

That I may walk in balance, equally male and female.

Queen Marie,

Bless me with the spirit of St. Maroon

That I shall never take for granted the freedoms that I have.

And with the light that emanates from

your Spirit, all darkness is Obsolete.

Holy Mother of New Orleans Voudou, pray for me.

Holy Mother of New Orleans Voudou, hear my plea.

Marie Laveau you are Queen of the Voudous,

please pray for me.

Ashé.

MARIE LAVEAU'S VÉVÉ

Vévés are sacred ritual symbols of the Voodoo spirits. Most of the spirits have their own unique symbols that act as conduits through which the spirit manifests in ritual. The symbol defines sacred space and serves as a loa's representation during the ritual. It is quite common for ritual symbols for a particular spirit to differ between temples, often variations on a common theme. Sacrifices and offerings are usually placed upon them. The vévé shown on page 97 is the one used in my temple and is similar, but not exactly the same as other versions of her vévé found in New Orleans.

In the past, vévés were thought to derive from the beliefs of the native Taino people of Haiti and were brought to New Orleans during the Haitian migration in the early 1800s. Current research suggests a link between the vévé and the cosmogram of the Kongo people.

Vévés are usually drawn on the floor using a powderlike substance, such as cornmeal, wood ash, red brick dust, gunpowder, or a blend of one or more of the aforementioned powders. In New Orleans, blessed chalk is used to draw vévés on sidewalks, walls, and the back of doors. The material depends entirely upon the rite, though cornmeal is a commonly used substance. Temple mothers often use their own secret blend.

Figure 17. Vévé drawn on the ground with chalk before Marie Laveau's tomb.
Courtesy of Jeffrey Holmes

Figure 18. Marie Laveau's vévé as drawn by the author.

While vévés are used in community ceremonies and temple congregations, they can also be used in individual devotion and conjure works. Gris gris bags, conjure pakets, and wangas are constructed on top of vévés associated with a particular loa to call that loa forth. Sometimes vévés are drawn on paper and then added to a gris gris bag or conjure paket to embed the gris gris with the loa's energy. Candles and magick lamps may be burned on top of vévés, and they may be drawn onto Voodoo dolls to connect the doll to the specific energy of the loa. Vévés are used in many ways in New Orleans Voudou whenever a Voudouist wishes to call the loa into their life.

You will need to study the vévé closely so that you can replicate it using cornmeal or chalk. I would suggest copying the image in this book using pencil and paper first. Draw the symbol repeatedly until you gain a bit of muscle memory and it starts to become automatic. It will take some practice, but with a little commitment you can do it. Once you gain familiarity with the symbol, you will then need to practice on the ground using a powder of your choice.

BLESSED CHALK

Chalk is a favorite medium for drawing vévés, sigils, crossmarks, and other ritual symbols in New Orleans. Chalk is also used in the Catholic sacrament referred to as "chalking the door" for the Epiphany house blessings. Thus, it is important to know how to consecrate chalk for ritual use as a Laveau devotee.

Figure 19. Kongo cosmogram.

To make your plain chalk blessed and ready for workin', draw a Kongo cosmogram and set your chalk smack dab in the center. Set four seven-day glass-encased candles on your altar at each point on the cosmogram. Pray Psalm 23 over the chalk each day until the candles burn all the way down. Now your chalk is blessed and ready for use.

VÉVÉ RITUAL

Performing a basic vévé ritual as a Marie Laveau devotee is simple. You will dress in white and go barefoot for this ritual. First, start with a clean space, either inside or outside. You will be spreading cornmeal around when you draw the vévé, so keep that in mind. Using Florida Water or Marie Laveau's Peace Water, cleanse the space by sprinkling a little of the liquid in the four corners of the room as well as the center. Take a pinch of cornmeal and make a crossroads in the air in front of you, then toss the cornmeal through the center of the cross. Alternately, draw three crossmarks in the air and toss the cornmeal through the center X. This creates a connection between the world of the Visible and the world of the Invisible.

Next, draw Marie Laveau's vévé on the ground using the cornmeal. Focus all your attention on the Voudou Queen as you create her visual portal. Once you have completed the drawing, place some offerings for her directly onto the vévé. Place a white or blue candle that has been dedicated to Marie Laveau in the center of the vévé. Pour a little water in front of the vévé. Then, kneel before the vévé, knock on the ground in front of the vévé, and call Marie Laveau's name three times. As you do so, tell her who you are, and sing her praises. Say a prayer asking her for assistance with your problem. Sit in quiet meditation for some time. It is a good time to do some divination using the oracle of your choice. Playing cards and throwing bones are traditional methods of divination in New Orleans Voudou. When you are done, scatter the cornmeal with your right hand and thank the Voudou Queen. Take a pinch of the cornmeal to anoint the top of your head and place a little on the tip of your tongue for blessings from the Voudou Queen.

Part Three

THE LAVEAU MAGICOSPIRITUAL LEGACY

Figure 20. Offerings of cigarettes and a Zulu-themed painted rock at the foot of Marie Laveau's tomb. Photo courtesy of Jeffrey Holmes.

Categories of Conjure in the Laveau Voudou Tradition

•••

Most indigenous religions contain a magickal or medicinal aspect that is intrinsic to that tradition. In New Orleans Voudou, the magickal traditions are referred to as Hoodoo (also referred to as conjure and rootwork) and gris gris. At some point in the early 1900s—likely spurred by both the onset of a viable commercial Hoodoo industry as well as practitioners going underground to avoid harassment and prosecution by the police—Hoodoo was separated from the community and religious aspects of Voudou and reduced to a stand-alone ethnobotanical folk magick tradition that spread throughout the country. A person could practice Hoodoo, conjure, and rootwork without working with the saints or spirits if they didn't want to. It was not necessary for conjure workers to be Voudouists; in fact, many conjure workers today are Christians and divorce themselves completely from Voudou. Interestingly, gris gris did not suffer the same fate as Hoodoo and has remained an integral part of New Orleans Voudou since Marie Laveau's time.

Hoodoo is an African American system of healing, harming, and protection. It relies on spiritual powers harnessed through ritual actions to affect change. Enslaved people used the system to cope with oppressive environments and harsh conditions, as well as a means of dealing with slaveholders and conflicts between members within slave communities (Fett 2002). Illness was often believed to be the result of conjuration and so finding forms of spiritual protection was necessary to achieve and maintain good health. Healing and harming methods were employed to establish dominance within a community, to exact revenge when necessary, to conserve resources, to seek justice, and to achieve balance. The system of healing, harming, and protection continued to serve folks post slavery as change was not at all immediate and the same basic human needs were present, whether one was enslaved or not.

Today, people will say that what Marie Laveau practiced was Hoodoo, not Voudou. I say what she did was Creole Voudou, which included what resembles Hoodoo today. The New Orleans Voodoo Museum differenti-ates the two by stating Voudou is what came from Africa while Hoodoo is an American-made phenomenon, born out of African tradition.[7] A more succinct explanation is that Hoodoo, like Voudou, has its roots in ancient African Dahomean cosmology and is connected to Legba and forest spirits called *Azzizas* who taught him the sacred use of herbs (gbo). Legba gave this knowledge to people in the form of a spiritual science—Hoodoo—that taught our Ancestors hand in hand with the Voudou spirits how to man-age day-to-day life and how to control and change one's personal destiny (Mama Zogbe, n.d.). As can be seen, the primary loa of New Orleans Voudou, Legba, is directly connected to Hoodoo (gbo). Despite this fact, the popular notion remains that "Voudou is a religion and Hoodoo is a magickal practice." That said, those who learn and practice the reductive Hoodoo that is separate from its religious counterpart, Voudou, are practic-ing a unique American tradition as described by the New Orleans Voodoo Museum. Those who practice New Orleans Voudou and Laveau Voudou are working within a unique African framework because the practice does not separate the Voudou spirits from the Hoodoo spiritual science. We acknowledge and embrace the two in their totality.

Years ago, I began to study the available literature for magickal activi-ties related to Marie Laveau to see if they matched up with present-day practices. In doing so, I observed a pattern of specific types of conjure workings emerge, so I placed them into categories. Though not exhaus-tive, I concluded the following twelve categories of conjure can be found in the Laveau Voudou magicospiritual lineage over time:

1. Bottle spells and container spells

2. Candle magick

3. Catholic conjure

4. Coffin conjure

5. Death conjure

6. Fetishism: doll baby conjure and ju ju

7. Front porch conjure

8. Graveyard work

9. Gris gris

10. Magick lamps

11. Supplications

12. Water rituals

Other forms of magick that Marie Laveau engaged in include knot magick and pillow conjure, as well as séances, which is not magick per se, but a Spiritualist practice that has persisted well into contemporary times. Due to space constraints, however, I opted not to feature them in this book. All forms of Laveau magick address activities of daily living, such as job security, love interests, court cases, healing, money, protection, and revenge. A mutual thread between categories is their shared religious and magickal origins. Voudou, Hoodoo, and conjure were "major forces in Afro-American spiritualism" whose "origins lay in West African cultures including the Yoruba, Dahomean and the Bakonga-dominated Kongo" (Armitage 2015, 90). Fetishism and bottle spells, for example, can be traced to these cultures. Gris gris originated in Senegambia and has been assimilated into present-day Laveau Voudou. Ancestor reverence (e.g., graveyard work) and water rituals are common to African cultures across the board. Catholic influences are evident in supplications, candle magick, and magick lamps, and a category unto its own I call "Catholic conjure."

In this section, I have featured twelve conjure categories and given examples of their use as reported by eyewitnesses and reporters during Marie Laveau's lifetime. I have also provided contemporary examples as well. Links to the historical record are provided to illustrate a continuity of practices within the tradition tracing back over a century, highlighting the Laveau magicospiritual legacy.

Bottle Spells
and Container Spells

•••

Bottle and container spells have their origins in the African Congo and Europe. Witch bottles, common in Europe, were used for a variety of reasons including healing from illness or injury believed to be caused by bewitchment (Manning 2014). Witch bottles were also used for more nefarious purposes, such as controlling someone, compelling them to a specific action, or to harm. For example, inserting a personal effect such as a target's fingernail clippings or hair in a bottle along with pins and broken glass would cause a sympathetic link to the target, causing them to suffer. In addition, witch bottles were used as apotropaic devices and were buried or concealed in the walls or fireplaces of homes to ward off evil and protect the home and its inhabitants.

The Marie Laveau tradition is filled with workings deployed via bottles, jars, and other containers such as cans and fruit. Unlike the European witch bottle that was often deployed for health reasons, bottle spells in southern conjure are mostly deployed in coercive and defensive magick. Bottle spells were reportedly among Marie Laveau's favorite types of conjure; she'd toss them in the river or bayou, or bury them in strategic locations, including one of New Orleans' many Cities of the Dead. She is also said to have left them at the doorsteps of enemies, breaking open bottles that contained asafetida, sulfur, and other smelly ingredients on the front porch to force the target to inhale her gris gris. This would create a panic in the person, as these strong smells stay "stuck" in the nose for some time and linger at the stoop. This surreptitious yet clever technique uses a type of magick

Figure 21. A bottle spell contained in the skull of a hog. *Courtesy of author*

called "contagious magick" and is a brilliant tactic in magickal psychological warfare. The smart conjure worker takes advantage of strong symbolism; whether or not a person believes in Voudou, society has conditioned people to fear material objects identified as such. Take the following example of the psychological effects of conjure caused by a vial of personal effects:

> The *Morgan City Review* reports a recent case of voudouism in that place which strikingly illustrates the influence of mind over matter, and the boundless reach of human credulity. The wife of a colored man named Brown had been confined to bed for ten months, suffering during that time excruciating pain. Believing that she was voodooed, her husband began searching for the "charm" and found a small four-ounce vial under the house, directly under the floor where the sick woman lay. Brown uncorked the vial; and it contained some of his wife's hair, a piece of her skirt, some new pins and needles, and a small quantity of fine earth. On the north side of a willow tree growing in the yard was cut the shape of a coffin, and a tack had been driven at the head, on each side, and at the foot, of the coffin. Brown cut away the mark from the tree and destroyed the

vial and its contents. In a few hours his wife was much better, free from pain, and the following morning she got out of bed and says she is about well. For months she had taken medicine, but it gave no relief, and the finding of the bottle and coffin mark had broken the voudou "charm" that had caused her severe suffering for so long a time (*Meridional* 1885).

Nowadays, sweet jars, sugar jars, honey jars, and vinegar jars are all the rage. In the olden days, the color of the sweetener used matched the race of the target. For example, brown sugar, honey, or maple syrup would be used to represent the hue of the individual's complexion. White sugar or clear Karo syrup would be used to represent white folks. This color symbolism is a form of sympathetic magick, providing a magickal link to the target by symbolically representing them in some fashion.

Sweet jars are used for any number of conditions in which you wish to have the edge: favorable court case outcomes, drawing a love interest, getting a job. On the other hand, vinegar jars are used to sour a situation, because vinegar is sour. In recent years vinegar jars have been renamed by internet conjure workers and witches as *sour jars*. As this is not the traditionally used name in New Orleans, I refer to them as my foremothers did, as vinegar jars.

SUGAR JAR TO GET A JOB

Sugar and sweet jars aren't just for attracting love interests. They can be used for any situation or condition in which you wish to draw something near, get a raise, receive a favorable court rendering, get paid time off, and even get a job. This sugar jar is based on a working described by a New Orleans spiritual worker in Hyatt's *Hoodoo-Conjuration-Witchcraft-Rootwork* in the 1930s (Hyatt 1970, 2:950). For this sugar jar you need the following ingredients:

- Clear mason jar
- Powdered sugar

- Cloves

- Allspice

- Nine white candles

- Image of the Sacred Heart of Jesus

- Paper and pen or pencil

Write your petition paper stating explicitly what you want. If it is a specific position with a specific company, name it. Write down all the benefits and hours you want, and write down personality characteristics of your potential boss. Fold the paper three times toward you. Fill the jar with the powdered sugar, cloves, and allspice, then add your petition. Close the jar and shake it up. Set the jar in front of the Sacred Heart of Jesus and set a white candle on top. Say something like, "Please soften the heart of (name of company or hiring manager), that he or she will offer me my ideal job with benefits and an agreeable supervisor." Allow the candle to burn down. Repeat this procedure for eight more days, burning a white candle on top of the jar each day, repeating your prayer.

SWEET JAR TO KEEP A LOVER CLOSE

This is an example of a sweet jar to keep a lover close provided by a New Orleans spiritual worker in Hyatt's *Hoodoo-Conjuration-Witchcraft-Rootwork* in the 1930s (Hyatt 1970, 2:949). It uses two containers: an apple and a jar. As a sweet jar, it is designed to literally sweeten a person to you—make them agreeable to you, attracted to you, loving toward you, or physically closer to you. This work can also be used to bring two people together in a romantic relationship.

This working should begin on a Monday. To make this sweet jar, you need the following:

- Wide-mouth jar (the jar you use requires a large, open mouth because you need to fit an apple inside it)

- Red delicious apple

- Karo syrup (the color used is determined by the complexion of the target individuals)

- Rock candy

- Pink candles

- Paper and pen

First, write the name of your target three times, once on three separate lines. Next, turn the paper 90 degrees and write your own name on top of the target's name three times.

Fold the paper three times toward you. Fill your wide-mouth jar with the appropriate sweetener halfway full.

Figure 22. Name paper as described in Sweet Jar to Keep a Lover Close.

Next, take a large red delicious apple and core it. Place the name paper inside the core, and then add some rock candy. Place the stuffed apple into the jar and fill the remainder of the jar with the sweetener. Close the jar.

Set a pink candle on top of the jar and burn it on Monday. Say the Lord's Prayer and ask God's power that this individual be kept close with peace, success, and happiness. Allow the candle to burn all the way down. Repeat two more times with pink candles on Wednesday and Friday. Keep the jar in a secure place in the bedroom.

VINEGAR JAR FOR JUSTICE

This vinegar jar is from the same New Orleans spiritual worker as the previous two sweet jars (Hyatt 1970, 2:953). It is designed to separate two people who are together but shouldn't be and who are going to court. This work is ideal for domestic violence cases where one partner would be better off leaving but has not left yet. It can also be used for a couple seeking a divorce. For this working you will need the following:

- Mason jar
- Red onion
- Paper and pen or pencil
- Copper penny
- Vinegar, warmed

Write a name paper similar to the previous work, only this time write their last name first. For example, *Lucious Lyon* would be *Lyon Lucious* and *Cookie Lyon* would be *Lyon Cookie*. The woman's name would be on top of the man's name in this case. In the case of same-sex couples, the person who is seeking victory based on righteous retribution would go on top of their partner's name. Fold the petition away from you three times.

Cut the onion into four quarters, but don't slice the onion all the way through. Stick the name paper into the onion along with the copper penny. Place the onion in the jar and pour the vinegar—which has been heated to a warm temperature—over the onion. Fill the jar with the warm vinegar, leaving an inch or two of space at the top. Close the jar and shake it up while praying, "If it is the will of God, then by the will of God may justice be served, and may this couple be put asunder." Keep the jar wrapped in a black cloth in a dark place, like a closet, where it will not be discovered by others. Every day it should be shaken and spoken to until the desired outcome is achieved. Once the issue is resolved, bury the jar in a cemetery.

Candle Magick

•••

In both Catholicism and Voudou, candles are lit for prayerful intentions; the flame holds the intention and symbolizes the prayer. There are numerous descriptions of Marie Laveau's altars illuminated with candles, and we even learn from witnesses how she lit her candles. She poured a liquid with high alcohol content into a saucer and "ignited it with a match . . . then, she took candle after candle, plunged them into the burning alcohol, and distributed them around, muttering mysteriously all the while" (*Times Daily Picayune* 1890, 10). Similarly, today's conjure workers pour Florida Water in a dish and ignite it. The burning blue flame of the alcohol is used to light the candles in the case of tapers and to cleanse the glass-encased variety with fire.

A power up to any kind of candle working that marries Catholicism and conjure is to light a candle in a Catholic church at the same time you are setting a light for healing or blessing for a client. Anyone can light a candle in a Catholic church, so don't be shy should the need arise. The flame will represent you and your prayerful intention long after you leave the church. Candles are used in all altar work and in the petitioning of saints.

When working with the saints, you will find the candle color corresponds with the clothing worn in the classic iconography. For example, artistic depictions show St. Anthony as typically wearing a brown robe; thus, his candle color is brown. Likewise, St. Jude's robe is green and so his candle color is green. One hard-and-fast rule is that when in doubt or when lacking a candle in a particular color, substitute a white candle for any other color. Just roll that white candle in some herbs, powders, and conjure oil, put your intention into that candle, and it will be every bit as effective.

Figure 23. Seven-day candles in a wall oven. *Courtesy of Jeffrey Holmes*

Like sweeteners, candle color was also associated with race in the past. White or pink candles would be burned to represent white people, while red represented brown folks. There are some references to the use of red candles to represent black folks and blue candles to represent brown folks in the Hyatt texts (e.g., Hyatt 1970, 1:801). Black candles were reserved for enemies without regard for race. It's a simple concept to follow, and these types of little tweaks were believed to enhance workings and even speed them up in certain cases. In this way, the old-timers followed concepts of imitative magick and the law of similarity in their conjure work.[8]

A final tip regarding candles from Marie Laveau. If you use taper candles or votives, save the nubs and wax remains when they burn down to add to your gris gris, unless the working specifically calls for disposal. As one witness to a Laveau Voudou ceremony observed, "The candles had burnt into tiny bits which were religiously preserved as potent factors in the gris gris" (*Times-Picayune* 1890, 10).

TO MAKE A LOST PERSON RETURN HOME

This working comes from a New Orleans practitioner referred to as "Gifted Medium" in Hyatt's *Hoodoo-Conjuration-Witchcraft-Rootwork* Volume 2. The work is supposed to find someone who is lost and bring back someone who is desired. For this working you will need the following:

- Red, white, and blue taper candles, one each

- Sugar

- Raisins

- Magnetic sand

- Fireproof saucer

Write the name of "[the individual who] desires de party" three times in a straight line on a piece of paper. Under the individual's name, write the target's name three times. Set the paper under the plate and fix the red candle to the plate by allowing some wax to drip on the plate and sticking the candle onto the wax until it hardens and is securely in place. Then pour some sugar around the candle, add some raisins, and on top of that, sprinkle some magnetic sand. This candle should be lit at nine o'clock in the morning. As it burns, you should call out the desired person's name three times, telling them to come home. Then at three o'clock in the afternoon, set the white candle on the plate and again, call out the desired person's name three times, telling them to come home. Lastly, at six o'clock in the evening, add the blue candle and repeat. Allow the candles to burn down. When the candles are finished burning, put the remnants of the work in a paper bag and bury under your front steps or front yard. If the working was performed for another person, give the bag of remnants to the person and instruct them to do the same. If you live in an apartment building or someplace without a yard, place the remnants in a red flannel bag and carry it on your person until the desired person returns home.

RITUAL TO GET SOMEONE OUT OF THE HOUSE

This ritual was reported to Zora Neale Hurston in her seminal work *Mules and Men* by a conjure doctor in New Orleans known as Father Watson, the "Frizzly Rooster." The working was recommended to a woman who had come to him complaining of "too many women in my house. My husband's mother is there, and she hates me and always puttin' my husband up to fight me. Look like I can't get her out of my house no ways I try. So, I done come to you" (Hurston 1935, 219).

After reassuring her, the Frizzly Rooster told her to do the following. Take a flat onion if the person you want to move is a woman, and a sharp-pointed onion if it is a man and core the onion out. Write the person's name five times on a piece of paper and stuff it into the hole of the onion, closing it up with the piece you just cut out.

Pay attention to the goings-on of the person and when they are leaving the house. One day, roll the onion behind them before anyone else crosses the doorway. As you are rolling the onion, make a wish for the person to leave the house. That evening take a red candle and burn it just enough to melt the tip. Cut the candle into three parts and place them in a glass of holy water. At midnight, go to the door of your target's home. Holding the glass in front of you, say, "In the name of the Father, in the name of the Son, in the name of the Holy Ghost." Shake the glass three times violently up and down, and after the last shake throw the glass to the ground and break it. Say, "Dismiss this person from this place!" When you leave that person's home, return to your home via a different route than the one you took to get there. That person should be gone within two weeks.

RITUAL TO MAKE A MAN COME HOME

This is a bare-bones ritual described by Zora Neale Hurston in her book *Mules and Men,* meaning Hurston omitted details needed to perform it successfully. As a result, I have filled in the blanks to complete the ritual. To cause a man to return home, take nine red or pink candles and wash them with Essence of Van Van. Then, inscribe his name on each candle using a brand new nail. Create nine name papers as described in the Bottle Spells and Container Spells section where you write the man's name three times, turn the paper 90 degrees to the right, and write your name over the man's name. Place the name papers under the candles, and light three candles at seven o'clock, three at nine o'clock, and three at eleven o'clock. As you light each candle, call out the man's name three times, compelling him to return home. Allow the candles to burn down and when they are finished, place the ritual remains in a paper bag and bury it under the front steps of your home, or in your front yard.

Figure 24. Agassou and St. Anthony, two syncretized spirits in Laveau Voudou. St. Anthony was a favorite saint of Marie Laveau. *Courtesy of author*

Catholic Conjure

•••

One of the defining elements of New Orleans Voudou and Laveau Voudou is the presence of Catholic elements and sacramentals. Not only do we see a variety of saints and manifestations of Mary, we also see Catholic-style altars, candles, crosses, and incense and a variety of psalms and prayers used. But let there be no mistake, Catholicism wasn't some sort of long-lost sister welcomed into the bosom of Voudou because enslaved folks thought it would improve their indigenous traditions. It was the result of the forced legal mandates of the Louisiana Black Code that "required all masters to have their slaves converted to Christianity within eight days of their arrival to the colony" (Desmangles 1990, 362). It was a strategic move by colonizers to further own people of African descent—and indeed anyone who was not Christian at the time—mind, body, and soul. Yet it was a move that ultimately backfired, because it provided an effective cover for African and indigenous traditional religious practices. Voudou afforded people a vestige of hope—a lifeline to what life looked like prior to slavery. There was just enough similarity between Catholicism and Voudou and the saints and the spirits that antebellum practitioners were able to continue practicing their beliefs under the guise of Catholicism. In the end, the hens in the henhouse outfoxed the fox, and Voudou in New Orleans survived.

Following are a few works that include Catholic elements. These types of works are characteristic of Laveau Voudou. Workers who are not Catholic may or may not perform these kinds of workings. Workers who are not Christian will not likely use these types of workings in their repertoire at all.

GOOD LUCK GAMBLING CHARM

In Catholic conjure and New Orleans Voudou, sometimes all that is required is the right prayer combined with a simple working. For a good luck gambling charm, write the Apostles' Creed backward on a piece of paper, then wrap the paper around a nutmeg fixed with Fast Luck Conjure Oil. Tie a green ribbon around it and anoint again with the oil. Carry it for good luck in general and in games of chance.

The Apostles' Creed Backward

Amen. Everlasting life the and

Body the of resurrection the,

Sins of forgiveness the,

Saints of communion the,

Church Catholic holy the,

Spirit Holy the in believe I,

dead the and living the judge to come will he and,

Father the of hand right the at seated is he,

Heaven into ascended he,

Again, rose he day third the on,

Dead the to descended he,

Buried was and, died, crucified was,

Pilate Pontius under suffered,

Mary Virgin the of born,

Spirit Holy the by conceived was who,

Lord our, Son only God's, Christ Jesus in believe I.

Earth and heaven of creator,

Almighty Father the, God in believe I.

BREAKING THE CHAINS THAT BIND YOU WITH ST. PETER IN CHAINS

The Feast of St. Peter in Chains recalls St. Peter's freeing from prison by an angel as told in Acts 12:3–19. In about the year 42, on the orders of Herod Agrippa, Peter the apostle was thrown into prison for preaching about Christ the Savior. In prison he was held secure by two iron chains. On the night before his trial, an angel of the Lord removed these chains from Peter and led him out from the prison.

The feast day of St. Peter in Chains is also known as Lammas Day, from the Old English *hlafmaesse,* for Loaf Mass. The name was applied to the feast because it was observed as an early harvest thanksgiving and loaves made from the new corn were blessed and distributed at mass.

St. Peter with chains symbolizes things being locked or unlocked, chained or unchained, blocked or unblocked, opened or closed, enslaved or free, among other things. As such, St. Peter in Chains can help you break through barriers that have kept you bound and stuck. Here is a recipe for St. Peter in Chains Bread you can make as an offering to him and eat in a ritualistic way to break the chains that bind you with his assistance. You will need the following ingredients:

- 1½ cups warm water

- 1 package yeast

- 1 tablespoon sugar

- 1 tablespoon salt

- 4 cups flour

- 1 egg (optional)

Dissolve the yeast in warm water. Add the sugar and salt. Mix in the flour and knead until the dough is smooth. Roll out dough and form into chain links. Connect the links to form a chain. Brush the dough with a beaten egg for a golden finish. Bake in a preheated oven at 425°F for 15 minutes.

Offer some bread to St. Peter on his feast day. He takes a red candle, as he is an apostle. Set some aside for yourself. Say the prayer for St. Peter:

Glorious chains! Never will you make St. Peter's successors tremble any more than St. Peter himself; before the Herods and Neros and Caesars of all ages you will be the guarantee of the liberty of souls. O holy apostle Peter, thou dost preside over the apostles by the precious chains which thou didst bear. We venerate them with faith and beseech thee that by thine intercessions we be granted the great mercy.

(State your petition).

Amen.

For each link of St. Peter's bread you eat, name it for an obstacle. Eating the obstacle symbolically gives you power and control over that problem so that you can move forward unencumbered. After three days, put the bread offering outside under a bush or a tree.

TO FIND A LOST PERSON

This working calls on St. Anthony to find and return a lost person. It is based on another simple working dating to the 1930s as described by a New Orleans spiritual worker in Hyatt's *Hoodoo-Conjuration-Witchcraft-Rootwork* Volume 2. You will need a brown candle, a white saucer, and an image of St. Anthony. To find a lost person, write your name three times on a piece of paper followed by the lost person's name three times underneath yours. Place the brown candle on a plain white saucer and set it before the image of St. Anthony. The petition paper goes underneath the saucer and candle. Light the candle and say, "I desire you to come, I desire you to come in peace." Rap on the table three times in front of St. Anthony and tell him to find the lost person (state his or her name) and to return his lost footsteps.

THE MAGNIFICAT

The Magnificat is a canticle, also known as the Song of Mary, the Canticle of Mary, and, in the Byzantine tradition, the Ode of the Theotokos. It is the hymn of praise by Mary, the mother of Jesus, found in Luke 1:46–55. It is traditionally incorporated into the liturgical services of the Catholic Church and of the Eastern Orthodox churches. But the Magnificat is more than just a prayer of praise—it also reminds us about the essential link between humility and holiness. It affords us the opportunity to examine our own actions and assess whether or not they serve to magnify the glory and goodness of God the Creator.

One of the most basic ways to protect yourself from all evil is to carry a copy of the Magnificat, written by hand on parchment paper and anointed with Dragon's Blood Ink or Fiery Wall of Protection Oil.

My soul doth magnify the Lord,

And my spirit hath rejoiced in God my Saviour

Because He hath regarded the humility of his handmaid: for behold from henceforth all generations shall call me blessed.

Because He that is mighty hath done great things to me, and holy is His name.

And His mercy is from generation unto generations to them that fear Him.

He hath shewed might in His arm: He hath scattered the proud in the conceit of their heart.

He hath put down the mighty from their seat, and hath exalted the humble.

He hath filled the hungry with good things, and the rich he hath sent empty away.

He hath received Israel His servant, being mindful of His mercy.

As He spoke to our fathers; to Abraham and his seed forever.

Glory be to the Father, and to the Son, and to the Holy Ghost,

As it was in the beginning is now, and ever shall be, world without end. Amen.

PALM FROND FOR PROTECTION

The palm is used in Christian iconography to signify victory of the martyrs or victory of the spirit over the flesh. This is why you will see images of martyred saints—such as St. Expedite—with a palm frond in hand. The palm branch is a symbol of victory, triumph, peace, and eternal life originating in the ancient Near East and Mediterranean. The palm was sacred in Mesopotamian religions, and in ancient Egypt it represented immortality. Palm branches symbolize the victory of the faithful over enemies of the soul. Palm trees and fronds are sacred in New Orleans Voudou due to classic Catholic and Christian symbolism, but also because of their connection with Father Père Antoine and his celebrated date palm tree.

This is an easy working for protection and blessings. All you need is a palm frond—ideally one procured from mass on Palm Sunday, but any one will work. Anoint the palm frond with olive oil and pray Psalm 23 over it. Hang it over the front door to keep evil and sickness away and bring blessings to the home.

PRAYER TO ST. JOSEPH FOR PROTECTION

This is a great prayer for Laveau devotees, as it seeks protection from one of the patron saints of New Orleans, St. Joseph. If you have a statue of St. Joseph, he can be kept in the living room or kitchen where he can keep an eye on the family for you. Burn green or white candles to St. Joseph. This prayer can be said to him daily for protection.

Gracious St. Joseph, protect me and my family from all evil as you did the holy family. Kindly keep us ever united in the love of Christ,

ever fervent in imitation of the virtue of our Blessed Lady, your sinless
spouse, and always faithful in devotion to you. Amen.

Anoint your statue of St. Joseph weekly with the purest olive oil so he can protect your family always. Feed him a paket of nine Guinea seeds contained in red flannel and tied around his waste. If you have an image of him, the paket of Guinea seeds should be kept behind the picture frame or image.

PSALM 23 SHOE CHARM

Psalm 23 is probably the most popular and commonly recited psalm in conjure work. It is used for any work with a positive intention. For example, it may be recited for blessings, abundance, prosperity, love, guidance, and protection. While it is often spoken aloud or silently to empower a working or while praying on behalf of a client, it is also commonly used in written form.

For this working, you need a standard size piece of paper with Psalm 23 handwritten on it. Alternately, you may print out a piece of paper with Psalm 23 repeated multiple times on it. Small font is good, so you have a lot of words on the page. Trace your shoes on the paper and cut them out. Fix the shoe cutouts with Devil's Shoestring Powder. This will literally trip up the devil should he try to hijack your footsteps and influence you to walk the wrong path.

I like to Modge Podge mine, because I find it preserves the shoeprints better. The idea is to leave the cutouts in your shoes when you are not wearing them to prevent any negative energy from attaching itself. When you put your shoes on, leave the cutouts in the exact spot where your shoes were. They will function as a decoy for meddlesome spirits that may be sent your way or that you may have unwittingly attracted. It is said that by the time those pesky spirits stop and count all the words on the shoeprints, you will be long gone and out of reach of the devil.

ST. JOHN THE BAPTIST WATER

To keep the law, bill collectors, landlords, and enemies away from your door, make some of Marie Laveau's St. John the Baptist Water.

On St. John the Baptist Day, June 24, fill a bottle with water from a river while reciting the Lord's Prayer. Lay the bottle on its side with the head of the bottle pointing out of the door. When the law is coming, or your landlord or any undesirable person, call out to St. John and Marie Laveau and ask them to help you keep the undesirables away. While doing that, take that bottle full of St. John the Baptist Water and roll it with your foot to the front door. If they come to your door, when they leave roll the bottle with your foot back to its position with the mouth of the bottle pointing out the front door. This bottle of water is to be kept from year to year and never emptied out.

Coffin Conjure

•••

One of the oldest and most traditional conjures attributed to Marie Laveau uses little black coffins coupled with a doll baby or gris gris. The trick entails placing a coffin containing a doll, usually made of black fabric and/or covered with a shroud, on the target's front porch. The coffin may be flanked with a couple of black candles and topped off with a gris gris bag for good measure. Coffin conjure marries the classic container spell with doll baby conjure and front porch conjure. It is not at all uncommon to find workings that combine elements of different classes of conjure.

Coffin conjure may or may not have death to the target as the goal. The intention could be to simply intimidate someone, or it may be to make an undesirable neighbor move. It can also serve as a warning to an abusive husband. It definitely seeks to end something, and it used to be so commonplace that there were newspaper articles written about it when it happened. It always served to psyche people out, which was half the intended fun for the worker. Take the following incident, for example, when two small coffins were found on the back steps of two residents in New Orleans:

> Last night, two small coffins were found on the back steps of two residents on Canal Street—the rear portion. These coffins were filled with black feathers in bunches and sulphur, emblems of the inferno. The residences were owned by poor people. The poor are sometimes too superstitious. This was to play on their superstitious feelings till they became alarmed and sick, and then have voudous summoned to avert the evil spell. The five dollars are the compensation. This is a bad time for these imps of darkness to try their infernal tricks.

Figure 25. A conjure doll in a coffin covered with a shroud. *Courtesy of author*

If they are caught they might be lynched. Let the Irish voudou use her whiskey, onions, cards and salt, if any choose to take them of their own free will. But these coffins, sulphur and feathers, charms bespeak an infernal design (*The Ouachita Telegraph* 1873).

TRADITIONAL NEW ORLEANS VOUDOU BLACK COFFIN SPELL

This spell is good for transformative magick, where the doll symbolizes the transformation of something negative into something positive, or the death of something old into something new, such as old ideas or habits into new ideas or habits. Perform this spell during a waning moon to remove an enemy, bad habit, or emotional distress from your life. For this working you will need:

- Black doll
- Photo of target
- Coffin
- Graveyard dirt
- Mullein
- Spanish moss
- Mugwort
- 3 black candles
- 1 lemon

Attach a photo of your target to the Voodoo doll with a black pin and write your target's name nine times on a piece of parchment paper. If you are seeking to stop a bad habit or resolve an emotional issue, write your desire on a piece of parchment paper and pin it to the doll. On top of and crossing the person's name or statement, write nine power words that describe your feelings for this person or condition, such as "wicked," "evil," "hate," "sick," etc. Attach the name paper to the doll with a black pin. Lay the doll in the coffin and sprinkle with graveyard dirt and herbs. Cut the lemon in half and squeeze the juice from both halves over the doll. Close the coffin with the lemons, herbs, and doll inside. Set three black candles on top of the coffin by dripping a bit of the wax on top of the coffin and sticking the candle into the melted wax. Light the candles. When they have burned down, take the coffin to a cemetery and find a tomb with a cross and bury the coffin under the closest tree to the grave or directly behind the headstone. Alternately, bury the coffin with a cross in the farthest left corner of your backyard.

COFFIN SPELL TO CAUSE THE DEATH OF AN ENEMY

This powerful coffin spell is adapted from Minta Owens, a conjure woman from New Orleans who was interviewed by Hyatt in 1938. She described a coffin spell designed to kill a person. Owens described getting a coffin, a doll baby, and three black taper candles that have been reversed and butted. To reverse and butt a candle, turn it upside down and carve to a point exposing the wick. Cut the point off the opposite end so it will stand correctly. Set aside.

Name the doll baby after the name of your target. Using holy water, splash a little on the doll's head and pronounce, "I now baptize you in the name of (your target's name). Let it be so." Write your target's name on a piece of paper and affix it to the doll. Set the doll inside the coffin and close the coffin. Light a black candle and burn it on top of the coffin on a Monday. While the candle burns, pray for the end of your enemy by saying, "In the name of God the Father, the Son, and the Holy Ghost, may (name of target) die." Repeat on Wednesday and Friday for a total of three times. Dispose of the coffin by burying it in a cemetery.

CIGAR BOX COFFIN

Nowadays, we can buy little premade coffins from craft stores to put our dolls and Hoodoo paraphernalia in. But back in the day, cigar boxes were used. Sometimes the boxes functioned as the coffin and in other cases they were used to contain another coffin and the box—which would be filled with graveyard dirt—served as a portable graveyard. So disguised, the cigar boxes could be brought into the home of the target before they would be aware they were being conjured. Cigar boxes make great makeshift coffins, as they are sturdy and cheap; you can purchase them from tobacco stores for a dollar or less in all different sizes. For this working, we are going to replicate the old-style conjure cigar box coffin.

The inspiration for this working comes from an 1874 *Times Democrat* article that describes a conjuration of Fanny Sweet, a woman who went by multiple aliases and had a notorious reputation for just about everything under the sun, including murder and prostitution. Apparently, she had an enemy or three. The article describes a cigar box discovered by a police officer on Fanny Sweet's front porch "covered with a white cloth . . . ornamented with leaves glittering in the flash of innumerable brass pins." On top of the box was a six-inch-long white coffin that contained the "mortal remains of Fanny Sweet, with a record of the day on which she was born and that on which she severed herself from her mundane connexions." The figure contained inside the coffin was made of dough with "pins bristled from her head and stood upright like the feathers of a Comanche Indian." At the four corners of the cigar box were "four vari-colored candles, and altogether it presented the appearance of a Liliputian wake." A note accompanied the gothic arrangement, addressed to Fanny Sweet herself, which was "couched in very expressive phrases," essentially cursing her to hell. The police officer took the box down to the station and informed Fanny of the discovery, when she reportedly went into hysterics due to being "in great trepidation about that Voudou," and was inconsolable, "having a strong belief in the infallibility of Voudou charms."

Figure 26. Sixth pentacle of Saturn from *The Greater Key of Solomon*.

With the above event in mind, procure a cigar box and set it aside. Purchase one of those wooden coffins from the craft store and paint it white. Grab some white cloth and brass tacks while you are there. Print out the sixth pentacle of Saturn and affix to the inside of the cigar box lid. Wrap the cigar box with the white cloth and hold the cloth in place by tacking it down with the brass tacks. You will have to cut the cloth to fit it snugly around the box and lid so the lid will be able to open and close. You can make a cross design or pentagram on the lid with the brass tacks if you wish. Fill the bottom of the cigar box with graveyard dirt. Close the box and set the coffin on top of the box.

Make some salt dough and fashion a doll from it to resemble your target (see the recipe for basic conjure clay on the following page).

Before you bake your doll baby, inscribe your target's name on the doll. If you wish to stick pins in it, do it before you put it in the oven. When you are done fixing your doll, place it into the coffin. Write a petition to set your intention and place it inside the coffin with the doll, then close it.

Set four black birthday candles at the four corners of the box and light them. Open the coffin. Say your target's name aloud, followed by, "Set thou

BASIC CONJURE CLAY

Here is a recipe for making a basic conjure clay from my book *Magickal Conjure Doll Clays:*

- 2½ cups flour

- 1 cup sea salt, kosher salt, or blessed salt

- 1 cup water

Combine the ingredients and stir until moistened. Add hexing herbs or banishing herbs to the clay, if desired, then mix until well blended.

Put on floured surface and knead until smooth, about 10 minutes.

Divide clay into several parts. Form into shapes ½- to ¾-inch thick. Use a cookie cutter if desired.

Bake on a greased cookie sheet at 325 degrees for 1 hour.

Dough can be refrigerated. Makes 10 to 12 doll babies.

a wicked one to be ruler over him and let Satan stand at his right hand." Allow the candles to burn down, then close the coffin and place it and the wax remains inside the box. Wrap it with a black cloth and keep it out of sight. Repeat once a month at the dark of the moon until you get the results you seek, then bury the box at a cemetery.

Figure 27. Example of a class of spell called "Killing Hurts." *Courtesy of author*

Death Conjure

•••

While Marie Laveau was known for her charitable works and Voudou healing rituals, she was also feared for her curses and death conjures. Most of these stories are retold with a sinister flair, but at least one of the stories may be considered a mercy killing.

Antoine Cambre, a prisoner sentenced to death for murder, was biding his time on death row at the Parish Prison where Marie did her ministry. She had been a regular visitor of his and "would cheer him up for hours with her lively conversation." She was chosen to erect an altar for him during his final days, and on the eve of his execution, she approached him and in her patois said, *"Ti moun, avant to mouri, si to dois mouri demain, dis moin ça to oulé mangé. Ma fais tois bon diner."* "Young one, before you die tomorrow, tell me what you would like to eat. I'll make you a good dinner." Too depressed to decide what he wanted for his final meal, he shook his head in resignation of his fate. In an attempt to comfort him, Marie said, *"Ma fais gombo filé comme jamais to mangé dans to la vie."* "I'll make you a gumbo filé such as you've never eaten in your whole life." And that is what she did. Marie made Cambre the most delicious gumbo he had ever tasted. A few hours after he finished eating, he was observed writhing in pain in his cell and not long thereafter he was dead. It was officially concluded that he died from a sudden attack of malarial fever, but the timing and circumstances led to the belief that Marie had poisoned him, sparing him the horrors of the gallows (Castellanos 1894).

Wishing for the ultimate demise of an enemy is a human inclination. Some would call it a weakness or a sin, while others call it something along the lines of righteous retribution. Death conjure may appear to be downright sorcery, and indeed, it can be. Nevertheless, it is not about simply destroying a person or relationship. In Voudou, its about balance and justice.

Another incident recounted in the newspapers was of a strange story of a Voudou curse by Marie Laveau on three women. Referred to as "The Fatal Sisters," it is a tragic story of the DeCourcey family, one of the wealthiest and most influential families in Louisiana before the Civil War. DeCourcey owned at least three sugar plantations, among them the famous Magnolia Plantation. When he was a young man, DeCourcey made the bold mistake of taking Marie Laveau's favorite granddaughter as his mistress. I have strong suspicions that this wasn't a mere affair and that when the story is told as "taking" her granddaughter, we may be talking about sexually assaulting her because of the depth and severity of the curse. It is said that Marie was so outraged she held one of her gris gris ceremonies on the shores of Lake Pontchartrain, summoned Li Grand Zombi, and "recorded the anthemas against the white master DeCourcey." Cursed in true Voudou fashion, "he would have no male heirs and his line should die with his daughters" (*The Republic* 1882, 2).

At first, no one took the curse seriously and it was laughed off as a joke, but over time, the story was well known by families all along the Gulf Coast. DeCourcey ended up getting married and had three daughters. But eventually the family succumbed to the curse of Marie Laveau. The father died, then two of his daughter's lost their husbands to duels, and another lost her husband to suicide. The curse of the Voudou Queen was fulfilled. All three husbands died violent deaths and all three daughters died without having any children. The DeCourcey family lineage was effectively eliminated.

Death conjure is a cultural reality and a fascinating aspect of the conjure tradition. While a lot of practitioners deny works of harm in Voudou, the fact is there are several different classes of works designed for harming and killing. These workings developed out of necessity from enslaved people needing to defend themselves from the abuses they endured. Many of these works are found in coffin conjure, fetishism, front porch conjure, and especially the gris gris tradition where poisoning was a very real threat. But Voudou is not the only tradition with death conjures. Ancient Greeks, for example, loved their curse tablets and kolossoi, dolls created to cause people grief and even death. This is part of human history across the globe.

In 2011, I made the first-ever videos of a class of death conjure called Killing Hurts. Part 1 illustrates the creation of two conjure doll babies and their preparation for the ant bed spell. Part 2 shows the dolls being consumed by ants. If you have not yet seen these videos, I highly recommend you take a few minutes to watch them on YouTube and then come back and read the rest of this chapter.[9] The working shown in the videos is further described in my book, *The Voodoo Doll Spellbook* (pp. 36–37).

Admittedly, watching a doll being consumed by ants can send shivers up the spine, but only if you have a limited perspective of the tradition. By the way, this kind of spell can be used for transformative and healing purposes as well. You can make a doll to represent a relationship you want to cut ties with, negative feelings you want to transform into meaningful ones, or a disease or illness you want to kill. Killing Hurts means a lot in Hoodoo—you can *kill* anything that *hurts*.

In the past, Killing Hurts was mostly done as revenge on a scorned lover. If a man or woman was carrying on with a lover while married, or if there was a couple that a person wanted broken up, then this kind of conjure was believed to work well. If someone wanted a person to disappear—and this can be interpreted as go away or die—then this kind of conjure was said to work. However, Killing Hurts could also be used for more positive purposes, as I have mentioned.

In conjure, we rely on sympathetic magick for which the basic premise is like produces like. In reading the tarot, for example, we know that pulling the Death card doesn't necessarily mean death. It can mean transformation or the death of something as opposed to someone. This same concept holds true with death conjure and Killing Hurts.

Let's say, for example, you have a problem with anger and you just can't seem to get it under control. You can create a doll and name it for your anger, put it on an ant bed, and let the ants help you destroy that anger. Or say you are grieving the loss of someone or are feeling emotionally stuck. Make a doll from cookie dough that represents your grief and stick it on the ant bed and ask the ants to help you transform the grief into healing. In a way, you would be using the trick as a sort of road opener or obstacle remover. This kind of working would be great to perform at a crossroads.

You can do this kind of work without the ant bed, of course, by simply burying the doll and letting Mother Earth take care of it. You can put a doll in a potted plant spell with a handful of earthworms and let the earthworms devour the doll. In this case, you would have to make sure the doll is made entirely of vegetable matter. You could then pot a plant on top of the doll and as the doll is consumed, so is your grief, anger, or obstacle. As the plant grows, so does the healing or transformation.

On the other hand, you could create a doll from plant matter that represents an enemy, and the very same working of planting the doll to decompose in the earth has a very different meaning. Or create a meat poppet and leave it out in the wilderness where an animal will consume it. Intention is key in magick.

Goophering (also goofering) is another class of death conjure. Growing up in the '60s and '70s in New Orleans, my only knowledge of the use of goofer dust was strictly for death conjure. So it was avoided, of course, and if you were exposed it was a serious situation. Nowadays, with the advent of the internet and influence of people from outside the tradition, goofer dust has been demoted to its use in harming. It is packaged and sold alongside graveyard dirt, love powder, and mojo bags. Personally, I do not sell it for ethical reasons.

FOR BAD WORK

This example comes from Zora Neale Hurston's *Mules and Men*. The working calls for the following:

- A coconut
- Beef gall

- Vinegar

- 15 black candles

Write the name of the person you want to get rid of on a piece of paper in the shape of a coffin. You can draw a coffin and write the name inside the drawing, if that is easier for you. Poke a hole in one of the eyes of the coconut and drain the liquid. Take the name paper and roll it up so that it will fit into the hole. Put beef gall and vinegar into the coconut, and write the person's name all over the coconut. Then stand the coconut in sand and set one black candle on top of it and light it. When the candle is burned down to a nub, light another candle and set it on top of the nub of the previous candle. Repeat this a total of fifteen times. The candle must never go out until the last candle is burned. When the last candle has burned down, place the coconut in a paper bag and bury it in a cemetery. The target should be gone shortly thereafter.

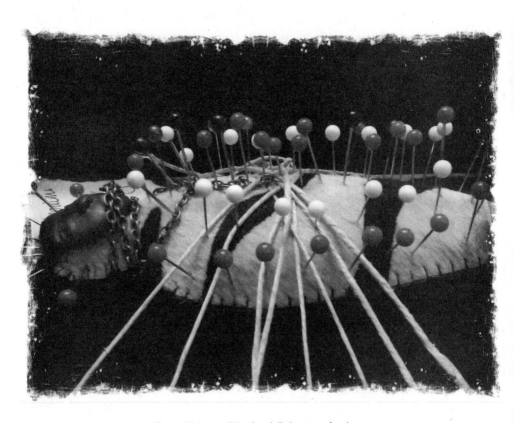

Figure 28. A cursed Voodoo doll. *Courtesy of author*

Fetishism:
Doll Baby Conjure and Ju Ju

•••

*The left hind foot of a rabbit killed in a graveyard in the dark of the moon
is a talisman of great virtue, and many are the intelligent people who
carry such charms about their persons.*

—TIMES-PICAYUNE 1895

Voudou has been referred to as a fetish religion since the first enslaved Africans arrived at the Americas with their ritual objects and talismans in hand. The term "fetish" derives from the Portuguese word *fetico,* which originally referred to "any work of art or such man-made religious objects as talismans, amulets and mascots which Africans, encountered by the Portuguese on their voyages, made use of" (Anderson 2015, 18). Many of the regions from where slaves were bought and sold have specific names for their fetish priests and priestesses and their ritual objects; however, Africans tend to describe them as "juju men" or "juju women." In New Orleans, fetishes are similarly referred to as "ju ju." Current studies suggest that the use of the word *fetish* to describe anything African is derogatory (Anderson 2015). While I acknowledge this sentiment, my use of the term is restricted to descriptions of ritual objects, is appropriate in the context of New Orleans Voudou, and is in no way meant in a derogatory fashion.

Fetishes are regarded as "spiritual, intelligent beings who make the remarkable objects of nature their residence or enter occasionally into images and other artificial representations which have been duly consecrated by certain ceremonies" (Puckett 1926, 171). Thus, there are two main aspects of a fetish: first, the object that acts as a container; and second, the indwelling spirit. The spirit is the essential part of the fetish as it must be called into the object for the object to have religious utility. It should be noted that the fetish spirit does not always live in its specified container unless it is instructed to do so by the ju ju priest or conjure worker. Further, since fetishes are viewed as alive with spirit, they must be fed in order to thrive. Feeding a ritual object consists of providing specific offerings at prescribed times, such as soaking a mojo hand in whiskey on a Friday. Not knowing how to feed a fetish can result in a "talisman, after being the source of luck" becoming "the cause of ruin and misery" (Métraux 1959, 291).

DOLL BABIES

Fetishes are described in the historical record, and we know through oral tradition that Marie Laveau often engaged in psychological warfare using doll conjure as a primary weapon. She would frequently create little dolls and place them on the doorsteps of enemies, and she used them to win court cases and to unite lovers, among other things. We also know dolls of various sizes and materials were present in Voudou ceremonies such as this one:

> In the centre of the table there was a cypress sapling, some four feet in height, planted in the centre of a firkin or keg. Immediately behind the cypress, and towering above it, was a black doll with a dress variegated by cabalistic signs and emblems, and a necklace of the vertebrae of snakes around her neck, from which depended an alligator's fang encased in silver (Buel 1883, 524).

JU JU

Fetishism in Voudou is not limited to dolls and wooden statuary. This aspect of the tradition often makes outsiders uncomfortable, and understandably so. Visitors to New Orleans will immediately notice alligator heads and paws, chicken feet, and bones of all sorts sold in curio shops. There is a cultural and historical precedence to the use of these types of items in New Orleans Voudou, as it is a direct holdover from the African Ju Ju tradition. These items were often used to contain ingredients designed to conjure a person, condition, or situation and continue to be used in a similar fashion by modern-day practitioners.

For example, the beef tongue rite remains a popular form of conjure, as is the use of chicken feet. However, a major difference between past and present practices is that animal sacrifice and killing animals simply for their parts in ritual is no longer practiced by most New Orleans Voudou practitioners. While this shift has been the subject of controversy by traditionalists from other African-derived traditions, who tend to look down on New Orleans Voudouists who do not embrace animal sacrifice as part of their practice, I personally only use ethically harvested animal parts in my conjure and do not practice, condone, or encourage animal sacrifice or the ritual killing of animals for magickal purposes. While Marie Laveau did practice animal sacrifice in the 1800s, it was a different time then, and I imagine beef hearts and tongues were more readily available than they are now. Her power was not and is not dependent upon the spilling of animal blood; it was always dependent upon her connection to Mother Mary, the spirits, the saints, and the Ancestors.

In Marie Laveau's day, it was not at all uncommon to find ju ju strategically placed throughout the city, often for sinister purposes. Take the instance of such a fetish that was found on a lot near the edge of a sidewalk in 1889 New Orleans. The whole fetish was presented on an altar—a boiled calf head with silver nickels in its mouth was set on a platter and placed on a small ladder with lighted candles, fruit, and other food offerings surrounding it. Whether or not the person for whom it was intended saw it is unknown, but apparently it did not garner too much terror: the man who first found it grabbed the coins, and a policeman simply kicked it into the street (*Johnstown Weekly Democrat* 1889).

Finally, we find references to black cat fetishism during Marie Laveau's lifetime and afterward. Robert Tallant in particular reported the practice of black cat sacrifice as a common occurrence in Marie Laveau's Voudou rituals, even devoting a chapter to it in his book *Voodoo in New Orleans*. My search for the truth regarding the prevalence of the practice almost invariably leads back to Tallant as the single cited source, so how common the practice was is still up for debate. However, there is a reference to black cat ju ju described by a teenaged boy who witnessed a Voudou ceremony while accompanying the family slave on a night out:

> Near where I stood was an oblong table about eight feet in length and four in width. On its right end stood a black cat, and on its left a white one. I thought them alive, and, having a certain fondness for cats, stretched out my hand to stroke the nearest. The touch, that most philosophical of all the senses, soon satisfied me that they were fine specimens of negro taxidermy (Buel 1883, 524).

From the above passage, we catch a glimpse of African fetishism and the memorializing of the black cat into a fetish and kept on a Voudou altar. The fetishized white cat is unusual; however, it makes sense in terms of spiritual balance.

Animal bones are popular ju ju among conjure workers. In the past, some of these special bones were procured in rather cruel ways. Again, it is unnecessary and cruel to kill an animal to procure a part for a working. If you can't find an ethical source for an animal part you think you need, then perhaps it is not needed after all.

BEEF TONGUE RITE FROM THE BOSS OF ALGIERS

The Beef Tongue Rite is performed when the goal is to silence someone who is gossiping or sullying your good name, or when you need to silence an opposing witness in court, among other things. It can also be used to curse someone, cause a separation or break up of a couple, or create general chaos and confusion in someone's life. There are many versions of the beef tongue ritual, and Harry Middleton Hyatt was able to record a few in *Hoodoo-Conjuration-Witchcraft-Rootwork,* including this one from a woman referred to as the "Boss of Algiers."

Note that this working is not for the squeamish, especially if you do not cook from scratch and never work with big pieces of raw meat or identifiable animal parts. However, it is a very popular working, and adherents swear by its effectiveness. For this rite you will need the following items:

- 1 large beef tongue
- 1 pound of grave dirt from the grave of an evil person
- 9 brand new needles fresh out of the package
- Paper
- Pen—a red pen if the target is white, a black pen if the target is black or brown
- Filet gumbo (powdered sassafras)
- Pepper—white pepper if the target is white, black pepper if the target is black or brown
- Red pepper flakes
- Cayenne pepper
- Tabasco sauce
- Spool of thread—white thread if the target is white, black thread if the target is black or brown

The specifics of gathering grave dirt are given by the Boss Woman. She states you must go on the evening of a new moon at six o'clock and locate a grave that is of a murdered person, someone who drowned, or otherwise died a sinful or awful death. Once the grave is located, which will require some research beforehand, dig at least 2 inches in the breast area and gather 1 pound of dirt. In my opinion, a pound of grave dirt is a lot and not necessary, but make sure to get a good amount. Refer to my book *Workin' in da Boneyard* for proper graveyard etiquette.

Place the beef tongue on a plate. Slice the tongue lengthwise down the center, but do not cut through it. You want it to remain intact and act as a container for other ingredients. Next, draw a human form on a piece of paper to represent the target. When you draw the form, include some identifying characteristics, such as a head of curly hair or glasses. Then write the target's name under the figure, and write it fifteen more times all around the figure for a total of sixteen times. Fold the paper up three times and stick it into the tongue, focusing your intention throughout the working.

Add the grave dirt, filet gumbo, peppers, and Tabasco sauce inside the tongue. Then take the pins and stick them all over the tongue. Some folks will use the pins to close the tongue, pinning one side to the other, alternating sides and crisscrossing the pins.

Finally, wrap the thread around the tongue, binding it up really good. Use the entire spool of thread to do this and tie securely. Place the tongue in a paper bag.

Take the whole tongue and bury it at the foot of a tree somewhere. It does not have to be at the target's home or anywhere near them. According to the Boss Woman, so long as it is buried at the foot of a tree somewhere, the spell will work.

BANISHING DOLL RITUAL

Here is a simple banishing spell that is believed to have originated with Marie Laveau. Marie Laveau's banishing spell is simple, yet classic in terms of New Orleans Hoodoo. For this spell you will need:

- Bottle
- Four Thieves Vinegar
- Parchment paper
- Small doll made from black cloth, or store-bought doll dressed in black

On a piece of parchment paper, write the name of the person you want to leave. Attach it to the doll and stuff the doll into the bottle. Fill the bottle with Four Thieves Vinegar and seal it. Throw the bottle into the Mississippi River or any moving body of water. According to legend, Marie Laveau asserts that as the bottle is carried away by the water, so shall this person be removed from your location.

Front Porch Conjure

...

In Marie Laveau's day, front porch conjure was a popular method of conjuring your meddlesome neighbor. When a worker wished to fix someone in a clandestine fashion, concealment of ritual objects under the front porch was the preferred method of deploying a working. Gris gris, bottle spells, black cats, and other items believed to possess the power to harm were often placed or buried under front porches. For example, when a file was placed under the front porch, "it will break peace forever—even make a man leave his wife" ("How to Conjure" 1899, 229). Similar accounts are documented of people finding strange substances on their front porches—crosses made of salt, black coffins with dolls in them, beef hearts wrapped in black crepe paper—and the message is clear: trouble is brewing!

In 1930, for example, an incident was reported by a couple in New Orleans known as Mr. and Mrs. Joseph Gautier. One morning the couple woke up to find a thoroughly moistened cross with a gris gris bag on top placed squarely in front of the door on their front porch. No one knew who put it there, though some of the neighbors swore they heard noises in the early hours of the morning on the day it was discovered. Though no one knew exactly what it was, Mr. and Mrs. Gautier thought twice before sweeping it away. In some ways, they were relieved it was just a cross of salt and not something more sinister. Hammond explains:

> A cross of salt does not mean death. A coffin with a name written upon it with a pencil dipped in vinegar would mean that, or an acorn stuffed with hair and bearing four holes in its sides; but a cross of salt means only trouble (Hammond 1930,12).

On another occasion, a "young white war widow" discovered a black wax "voodoo cross" on her doorstep. The cross had the woman's name inscribed on it, with forty-three pins stuck deep into the wax. At the top of the cross was a string with nine knots in it. It's hard to say why there were forty-three pins specifically; my first thought was it could be the target's age, but as she is identified as young, that would seem to rule out that idea. Perhaps it is directed at her lover? Knotted strings are a common working in Hoodoo. The number nine is considered a powerful magick number, and with each knot tied a prayer or intention is spoken. Each knot is also typically anointed or fixed with some sort of condition oil, meaning the oil would have been consistent with the condition or purpose of the working. Sometimes, knots are fixed with a lover's semen or vaginal juices in spells designed to dominate or control someone's nature, which is Hoodoo-speak for keeping a lover faithful. The newspaper stated the cross "symbolized death or separation from friends," while the police stated it was "an attempt to extort money." Locals said it was likely designed to "turn the young attractive woman against a boyfriend" (McClean 1949). While it's impossible to definitively interpret any remote working from another century, the fact that the cross was stuck with forty-three pins strikes me as overkill. It reflects an obsession of sorts, like when murderers continue to stab their victims over and over again long after they are dead. "That's reserved for real mean 'hoodooing.' That's when you're so mad at somebody you want to pull out all the stops" (McClean 1949). It demonstrates a real anger and fills a complex psychological need to not just stop or control a person, but to inflict serious injury. It's the sort of thing that drives crimes of passion, only with Voodoo, nobody is actually stabbing anyone.

Sometimes, objects found on doorsteps and front porches were not placed there for nefarious purposes. Rather, they were intentionally placed there as a means of bringing good luck or protection to the family residing in the home. The ritual object may be placed by the homeowner or family member, or it could be placed there by a conjure worker for hire.

Now, you may be thinking, good thing this sort of conjure is a thing of the past. But you would be wrong. People still engage in this kind of ritual behavior and will continue to do so as long as there are commercial spiritual enterprises and perceived competition between business owners. Just this year, for example, one business owner found a mess of fish and chicken feet dumped on their business's doorstep. As symbols of abundance, prosperity, happiness, endurance, fertility, health, creativity, and more in life, leaving dead fish would symbolize the loss of all of the positive attributes of the fish. It can also signify great losses and disappointments to come.

Clearly this event was done as a warning by a rival business owner or someone else in the community who disapproves of the targeted business. That said, the items and the way they were left leave me to suspect it may or may not have been done by a conjure worker. The fish are laden with Christian symbology and chicken feet are typically a good thing to Voudous and Hoodoos. They are not what we would think of as a jinx. In fact, they are useful allies. Chickens are believed to be protectors and frizzly chickens are skilled in scratching up conjures in the yard. Chicken feet are used as good luck ju ju and are believed to ward off evil and negativity. In one sense it seems like someone who has access to fresh fish and raw chicken feet just decided to grab some random "scary-looking" raw animal parts and dump it, counting on the psychological impact it would have on the targeted business owner. Without knowledge of how things work, the person may have actually designed a jinx that is nullified by the presence of so many chicken feet.

Pouring animal and fish parts on an enemy's doorstep is a long-standing conjure practice that can be traced back to the 1800s. In 1879, for example, a woman named Mrs. Mathe who lived on Dumaine Street in New Orleans was convinced there was a Voudou who wanted to annihilate her and her family. The "wickedly inclined woman, whoever she may be, while Mrs. Mathe and her family were asleep, went to her residence and covered the steps leading from the street with oil, teeth of animals, horses' hair, herbs, and fins of fishes" (*New Orleans Daily Democrat* 1879). When this conjure apparently didn't work, the Voudou returned and doubled up on her front porch conjure leaving coal tar, candles, a coffin, and a skull. While Mrs. Mathe stated she was not a believer in Voudouism, "she was terribly shocked, and nothing could persuade her to believe but that it is the forerunner of some terrible catastrophe that will happen to either herself or to some member of her household" (*New Orleans Daily Democrat* 1879).

While front porch conjure still occurs in contemporary society, new technologies present new challenges in successful deployment. In 2017, for example, there was the case of a spiritual attack in the tradition of front porch conjure on Hearthside Candles & Curios in Ralston, Nebraska. Shop owner Alex Fernandez arrived to work one day, only to see a pile of suspicious looking stuff—no doubt gris gris—on the front doormat of his shop. He proceeded to spend the afternoon reviewing his security footage and it showed a man dumping something from his bag in front of the door. Not only that, he recognized the perpetrator.

The event left Fernandez somewhat baffled. "We are a metaphysical shop, and this was kind of the metaphysical equivalent of leaving a dead fish on someone's doorstep. It's meant as a threat," Fernandez stated in an article for KPTM News in Nebraska. He says that threat was meant to bring bad luck to his business and to cause customers to cease from visiting his establishment.

"The fact that this person would do this and get caught doing it is just pretty stupid," Fernandez said. As a result of the attack, Fernandez focused on stepping up security and installed a new surveillance camera (Saunders 2013).

This latter example really drives home what not to do as a Hoodoo in an urban environment. There are security cameras everywhere now. You cannot disregard this fact and expect to perform a clandestine work and go undetected. You have to assume you are being watched. Given this fact, you may want to disguise your appearance. Unless you want to be caught and your identity known, then you must strategize your attack in a way that addresses today's realities so that a conjure working designed to be covert and clandestine, is deployed in a way that insures its covert, clandestine nature.

RED BRICK DUST

No doubt the most well known of protective front porch conjures in New Orleans is red brick dust. Red bricks can be seen all over New Orleans, from the old brick streets to the brick graves in the Cities of the Dead. New Orleanians have found a variety of esoteric uses for them, but the most commonly known use for red brick dust is its application in pulverized form to the front steps of the home as a means of keeping evil away. Since Marie Laveau's day, red bricks have been plentiful and can be procured all over the city.

The use of red brick dust has been mentioned in a number of writings. In *The Life and Works of Marie Laveau*, for example, Raul Canizares talks about hex-proofing the home Orleans-style:

> New Orleanians since before the time of Marie Laveau swear by the power of red brick dust to ward off evil. Simply get an old red brick, hammer it to dust, and spread the dust around the front of your house, using a broom. Keep a pan of water that has been treated with a ball of Indigo bluing (anil) behind your front door, and draw crosses using cascarilla behind every door of the house. Add a couple of drops of urine from a child and use the mixture as a floor wash, this will complete making your home hex-proof (Canizares 2001, 23).

To hex-proof your home using red brick dust is simple. Simply find a red brick—the older the better, because older bricks are softer than newer ones. Then crush it to powder using a hammer. Spread the dust across the threshold of your home and no evil will be able to enter.

Figure 29. Offerings left for Papa Guédé at a graveyard. *Courtesy of author*

Graveyard Work

•••

Working in cemeteries is common for New Orleans Voudou and Laveau Voudou practitioners and reflects the ancestral nature of the tradition. Working with Ancestors and hiring spirits, burying tricks, and gathering graveyard dirt are some of the usual activities taking place in graveyards. I've known some sorcerers who like to get high and have sex after midnight in cemeteries to gather power from the willing spirits and energies there, but don't think anyone will talk to you about it. A sorcerer can gather the dirt from under the place where they had sex, which could be on the grave of a spirit with whom they have made a contract, or on the ground. The dirt is then used in future works of sex magick and domination, in particular. Graveyard dirt in general is a staple ingredient in the medicine/medzin chest of any rootworker and is used in spells of justice, revenge, gambling, luck, and healing. Practitioners of Laveau Voudou carry on the tradition and are known to work in cemeteries for all sorts of workings, even for love and sex!

Marie Laveau is reported by Louisiana Writers' Project informants to have worked in multiple cemeteries. One such informant, Anita Fonvergne, recalled Marie Laveau "used to go to this tomb in St. Louis Cemetery No. 2 to do her private or her bad works . . . I don't know whose tomb that was where Marie worked, but I guess it was some woman like herself" (Breaux 1939). Marie Laveau is also known to have worked in St. Roch Cemetery in New Orleans for court cases and legal issues. St. Roch Cemetery is part of New Orleans' sacred geography because of Marie Laveau's connection to it, as well as because Doctor John Montenee is buried there.

There are a few precautions to take prior to entering a cemetery for conjure work. Always knock on the gate and ask permission to enter. Leave fifteen cents in silver coins at the gate as an offering. Some folks will bring protective talismans with them and cover their heads to protect evil spirits from entering their soul. For a detailed discussion about working safely in graveyards, please refer to my book *Workin' in da Boneyard*.

COURT CASE CONJURE IN ST. ROCH CEMETERY

Oral tradition tells us that Marie Laveau often worked her conjure in cemeteries and provided her clients with instructions to do the same in certain instances, especially in her latter years when she was bedridden due to failing health and could not accompany them. One worker from New Orleans, identified as the cousin of a Hoodoo doctor named Julius P. Caesar, described how Marie Laveau went to St. Roch Cemetery for court cases and legal work. Hyatt incorrectly identifies Julius P. Caesar as a white man, but his cousin stated, "He was colored and he was well-known there" (Hyatt 1970, 2:1642). Julius P. Caesar's reign was somewhere around the turn of the century. Indeed, a little research reveals that Caesar—known in the city as the "King of the Hoodoos" for thirty years—was actually arrested in 1902 for practicing as a "magnetic healer" in violation of a city ordinance against magnetic healers and fortune tellers (*Times Democrat* 1894). His arrest says little about his efficacy as a worker, though; at the time the city was in the midst of a campaign to crack down on mail order fraud and disproportionately targeted and imprisoned people of color who sold spiritual cures and charms (Long 2001). In any event, Caesar's cousin recounted how Marie Laveau would help with legal issues:

> If you went to her for a lawsuit case, or if a fellow had killed another person, and you'd go to her and tell her, "Well, my brother done kilt a man and he killed him in cold-blooded murder and I want to find out what can be done about it," she say, "Well, you got to go out to St. Roc, St. Roc graveyard."

. . . She'd go and make her wish there—you there with her—and when you'd go on back out there, she'd quite naturally get the name of the judge, the district attorney whosomever he is, and she'd go ahead on back and she'd fix up a little bag and put it on you, or else she would get in with the police, give him ten or fifteen dollars, tell 'im, "Now you get this to so-and-so-and-so." She was pretty well in with them. And theys go there and hand it to whosomever in jail, and he put that in there, and it wouldn't be nothing but mistrial, mistrial, mistrial until it makes the judge just get mad and discharge it. The case never come up (Hyatt 1970, 2:1648).

To actually work a court case in the graveyard like this would entail a few activities left out in the above description, such as hiring a spirit to assist with the work and/or buying graveyard dirt. Now, there are a number of ways in which to hire a spirit and even more reasons for doing so. However, since Marie took her clients into the graveyard with her "to make a wish," I am going to describe the least complicated and safest version of this kind of work.

To be perfectly clear, this is advanced graveyard conjure. To hire a spirit to assist you in conjure requires making a contract with the spirit. Now, don't let this scare you; you aren't selling your soul! But if any of this gives you cause for concern, do not do it. In fact, the best thing would be to go with an experienced worker who can walk you through it safely. At the very least you should read *Workin' in da Boneyard* before venturing out into the great ghostly beyond.

If you live in or around New Orleans, you could easily access St. Roch Cemetery and do the ritual there just like Marie Laveau did. If not, you can substitute any accessible cemetery for the work.

First, you will need to locate the grave of a lawyer, judge, attorney general, police officer, politician, or someone who was in a position of legal authority when they were alive. In Hoodoo, specific power and energy is accessed through graves that have specific associations. For example, for healing works, grave dirt from a doctor, nurse, or medic is ideal, while the graves of bankers and the wealthy are ideal for money workings. Of course, one of the best graves of all is that of a known conjure worker or Voudou Queen. It used to be easier to locate these kinds of graves in New Orleans, but the Church removed the grave markers "not because they practiced Voudou but because people were vandalizing the sites" (McConnaughey 2015). Finding the right grave will require planning, so do your research and take your time. Once you have located the ideal grave, you will be able to return to gather more for future cases—so it is important to get this step right.

Once you locate an appropriate grave, spend some time there visiting. Tidy up the grave if it needs it. It is important to listen carefully and be observant. Sometimes you will hear a mourning dove or a crow caw. These are good signs. If it feels right to you, then proceed. If it doesn't, move on to another grave.

When you find the right grave—one that feels comfortable to you and welcoming—then tell the spirit who you are and what you need. Do not say the person's name to whom the grave belongs out loud lest they follow you home. This can be problematic for anyone, even for the very skilled conjure worker. I recommend spending time at the graveyard and visiting the specific grave a few times before ever bringing someone else there.

Once you feel like you know the spirit and have developed a relationship with a degree of familiarity with them, then you can bring a client there and petition the spirit for assistance. Take your client to the grave and introduce them to the spirit of the grave. Make your offerings of fifteen cents and some rum, and have the client bring offerings of water, flowers, and fruit or pastries. Have them make an X on the ground before the grave and state their petition. When they are done, thank the spirit for listening and for their help, and leave the cemetery.

Next, you will return to the cemetery alone to gather some dirt from the grave site. In some cemeteries in New Orleans this can be tricky if the grave is in an aboveground tomb or wall oven. So, keep this in mind when locating a grave for ongoing work.

Ask permission to gather some dirt from their grave and tell them why you need it. Make an offering of fifteen cents in silver coins and a small bottle of rum as payment for the dirt. Tell the spirit what you are leaving as offerings and why. Then, using a knife or small shovel, gather some dirt. Take dirt from the place where their right hand would be, if it is that kind of grave. This represents the Right Hand of Justice. If not, gather the dirt from wherever you can. Small rocks and pebbles are also good to gather. You are going to make a gris gris for your client with the dirt.

Thank the spirit and leave the cemetery.

Like Marie Laveau, you will want to find out the name of the court, the presiding judge, names of the opposing parties, and any other relevant information about the case. Write down the names and their roles, and state what you want them to do with regards to the case. You must be very specific. Don't forget to write down the name of your client as the person for whom the conjure is performed. This will be your petition. It should be a statement of outcome of the case.

For the gris gris, fold the petition and add it to a red flannel bag. To this, add the grave dirt you gathered, a piece of Low John root, Solomon's Seal, Deer's Tongue, and a black-eyed pea. Add a few drops of Black Candle Tobacco Oil or Court Case Oil to the gris gris bag and tie it closed. Pray Psalm 5 over the gris gris five times before giving it to your client. Once you give it to your client, tell them to add a personal effect of their own to the bag, such as some hair or nail clippings, and keep it on the right side of their body straight up until the court date. The client should be instructed to recite Psalm 5 daily over the bag and anoint the bag weekly with an appropriate conjure oil.

GRAVEYARD LOVE RITUAL

This ritual is performed in a cemetery at the grave site of a married couple. You are going to call upon Baron Samedi, the Voudou loa of Death, magick, and sexuality to empower the working. So, the first order of business is to have a graveyard where you can work uninterrupted. If this is not possible, then you shouldn't attempt this ritual.

You will need the following items:

- Framed photograph of the people to be united in love

- Incense burner or brazier

- Charcoal

- Incense blend—myrrh, rose petals, lavender, sage

- Feather fan

- Pink and red flowers and a vase to put them in

- Florida Water

- Image of Baron Samedi or a skull to represent him

- White rum

- Patchouli oil

- New nail

- Lovers candle or Adam and Eve candle

Locate Baron's grave, which will be the biggest cross in the cemetery or the oldest male grave. Offer him fifteen cents and some rum and ask him to help you with a love ritual. Just talk to him and tell him what you are doing and what you need. Ask him to guide you to the right grave site to work at—you want a site where a husband and wife are buried side by side or in the same tomb or crypt. Once you locate the ideal graves, ask the spirits of the graves if it is okay that you perform a love spell there. Tell them you just need their space and permission to work there. You will not be asking them to work the conjure for you. If they are agreeable, offer them each fifteen cents and some rum. How will you know they are agreeable? You will have to be patient and feel. If it doesn't feel right for whatever reason, do not proceed with the working.

Then, prepare the space. Create a little altar in front of or between the grave sites. You will have to be adaptive based on the kind of graves you are working with. Set up the photograph of the couple to be united in love. Place the skull or image of Baron Samedi next to the photograph. Take the candle and inscribe the names of the couple into the candle with a new nail. Anoint the candle with patchouli oil. Set the incense burner or brazier in front of the photograph and light the charcoal. Sprinkle some of the incense onto the charcoal and get a good smoke going. Fan the smoke over yourself, then the graves, the skull or image of Baron Samedi, the candle, and lastly, the photograph. As you smoke the photograph, say, "With the resurrection of the body and life everlasting, Amen." Pour a libation of white rum in front of the graves.

Sprinkle the flowers with the Florida Water and then touch them to the photograph three times. Say, "I call on the orishas, the loas, and the Ancestors. I call on the supernatural powers of the Dead. I call on the guardian angels of (names of the couple to be united) and the Voudou Queen Marie Laveau to bring them together in love and happiness."

Touch the flowers to the fixed candle. Light the candle. Call out the names of the couple to be united nine times followed by, "Holy spirits of the dead, I ask your assistance in uniting this couple in everlasting love. So it is, so shall it be."

Set the flowers in the vase. Allow the incense to burn completely. Collect the skull and incense burner and the rest of your items after the incense has finished burning and leave the photo and flowers. Thank the spirits and Baron Samedi as you leave the cemetery. After nine days, you may retrieve the photo and candle remains and leave a small offering and fresh flowers. Wrap the photo in a red cloth and give it to the couple in the photograph.

Figure 30. A gris gris bag made from leather and sewn shut. *Courtesy of author*

Gris Gris

•••

Of all things Voudou, Marie Laveau is perhaps most famous for her gris gris. People from all walks of life went to her for advice, guidance, and a little mojo regarding their relationships. Remember the story about the young man who had been falsely accused of raping his girlfriend? Well, there is another part to that legend. About a year after having won the case, that young man went to Marie for help. He was lovesick. He wanted desperately to be with the girl, but she would have nothing to do with him due to pressure from her family. He told Marie that he couldn't bear to live without her. He told her he didn't have any money but that he would give Marie everything he had if only she would help him win back his girl's heart. Marie agreed to do the work pro bono if he agreed to be her informant. About what, nobody knows for sure, but given the girl's elite social status, I'm sure Marie had her reasons for wanting a little *kompromat* on the family.

Marie fixed two gris gris bags and instructed the young man to put one under the girl's doorstep and to carry the other one with him, especially when he attended the same Sunday mass as she. He faithfully attended church every week, and after seeing him at all the services for about three months, she approached him one day and asked him to marry her. The gris gris had worked.

According to the historical record, gris gris predates the introduction of Voudou in New Orleans. It is a system of talismanic magick originating in West Africa. Because the word *gris* means "grey" in French, it is incorrectly assumed that the word is French in origin. On the contrary, the etymology of the word *gris gris* actually derives from the Mande language group in what is today Senegal and Mali. Gris gris, along with other African religious systems such as fetishism and ju ju, became enmeshed with and a defining characteristic of New Orleans Voudou.

Historically, gris gris comes in a myriad of forms. It can be a powder, a liquid, poison, words written on paper, or botanical, mineral, and zoological items in a bag. In contemporary New Orleans, gris gris bags are the most commonly known and are essentially a means of carrying a charm, prayer, or spell. They are a favorite among tourists, who commonly seek charms related to love, money, luck, and revenge.

Traditionally, gris gris may be worn around the neck on a leather cord, around the waist in cases of infertility, and around the head, arms, or ankles according to the condition of the patient. They are contained in elaborately etched or plain leather pouches that have hand-sewn or handwritten text from the Koran inside, along with special numbers with mystical meanings. They are blessed with holy water, and specific prayers are said over them before they are given to the wearer. The marabout directs energy released through the spoken word toward a specific end. This energy is consequently attached to the gris gris amulet, which may be held in secret or displayed publicly (Alvarado, 2011). In New Orleans Voudou, it is customarily recommended that individuals keep their gris gris in the pocket or bra, on the right side if a man, and on the left side if a woman.

Finally, traditionalists in New Orleans Voudou will use both leather and flannel to hold their gris gris. Instead of verses from the Koran, many will substitute hand-drawn talismans, psalms from the Bible, or chants and words of power codified in one of the magickal alphabets from European magickal traditions. In New Orleans, the Theban or Witch's Alphabet is among the favored of these alphabets.

GRIS GRIS AS VOUDOU RESISTANCE

Voudou in all forms has historically been considered to be a form of cultural resistance to colonialism and oppressive governments and has even been specifically accessed by practitioners as a class of mystical warfare. In colonial times, the successful use of specialized esoteric spiritual knowledge by slaves in warfare and insurgencies gave the ruling white minority wherever slavery existed a reason to fear Africans and their descendants. These fears were confirmed with two events that threatened the slave institution: Makandal's Conspiracy in San Domingue in 1757–1758 and Tacky's Rebellion in Jamaica in 1760 (Bellegarde-Smith 2005).

Originally believed to be from West Africa, François Makandal was an enslaved runaway and rebel leader in San Domingue, who claimed to have supernatural abilities. He had extensive knowledge of plants and herbs and the ability to make poisons. His reputation for having advanced skills in botanical medicine coupled with supernatural abilities helped him to successfully organize different Maroon groups and coordinate their resistance activities. He and his followers effectively poisoned plantation owners, other enslaved people, and even animals. Authorities feared that Makandal had the initiative, plan, and means to kill all the white people living on the island. Before he officially launched an out-and-out rebellion, Makandal was apprehended and condemned to death in January 1758 at Cap-Français. The plan was for him to burn at the stake, but when the fire was lit he broke free and ran off, an event that amplified his legendary status. Makandal was immediately recaptured, however, tied to a new board, and successfully set on fire (Colonial Williamsburg Foundation 2019).

Tacky's Rebellion, an uprising of Akan (known at the time as Coromantee) slaves, was so impactful it blew people's minds. Tacky, the leader of this revolt, had been the king of his village in Fante land, West Africa. Tacky had the support and cooperation of local Obeah men who dispensed a powder to combatants that was designed to protect them from injury in battle. The powder, coupled with the belief that Obeah men could not be killed, fueled insurgents' confidence in the fight. Tacky and his followers cleverly began their uprising on Easter Sunday when they knew no one would be paying attention or suspect anything. They easily took over several plantations and killed the owners. When they stopped for a break to celebrate their success, a slave snuck off and ratted them out. Shortly thereafter, a mounted militia of seventy to eighty men, along with a group of Maroons who were bound by treaty to suppress such rebellions, arrived to put a damper on the party. They captured and murdered an Obeah man by hanging him "with his mask, ornaments of teeth and bone and feather trimmings at a prominent place visible from the encampment of rebels" (Evans 2004). This caused many of the rebels to lose confidence and return to their plantations.

Tacky and his followers were chased by the Maroons, and the legendary Maroon marksman known as Davy shot Tacky, cut off his head, and displayed it on a pole in Spanish Town. The rest of his followers were found in a cave near Tacky Falls, having killed themselves rather than succumb to slavery. While this particular insurgence was stopped, it prompted a series of other rebellions to break out all over Jamaica. Tacky's Rebellion occurred in Jamaica from May to July of 1760.

Of course, the most frightening instance of warfare won by Voudou was the Haitian Revolution. Louisianans greatly feared the Haitians coming to New Orleans because of this legendary historical event. During and after the war, swaths of refugees made their way to New Orleans, bringing their ancestral traditions with them. This is when Haitian Vodou met the Voudou-rich milieu thriving in underground New Orleans.

The growing instances of slave revolts in the Caribbean made authorities in Louisiana paranoid. A prime example of this can be seen in the infamous "Gris Gris Case," which occurred under Spanish rule in 1773. Authorities caught wind of slaves attempting to murder their master using a type of poisonous gris gris. The fear was that they would succeed, and instigate a rebellion against the slave institution, so the men were taken to court and tried for conspiracy to commit murder (Frieberg 1980).

RITUAL BLESSING OF THE GRIS GRIS

This is a ritual for blessing gris gris that you have already created, or gris gris in the raw, such as found insects, snakeskins, or other items intended to be used as gris gris. This ritual comes from a description of Marie Laveau conducting a ceremony where she petitions Li Grand Zombi in the making and consecrating of gris gris. In the ceremony she is calling the spirits into the gris gris and uses candles and the flames of burning alcohol to accomplish the task.

For this working, you will need:

- 2 candles in the color appropriate for the intended use of the gris gris

- Gris gris

- Fireproof saucer

- Florida Water

- Matches

- Wooden box

- Snake figurine to represent Li Grand Zombi

First, create a little gris gris altar. Place the snake figurine in the center and two candles on either side of the snake. The saucer goes in front of the snake. Pour some Florida Water into the saucer. Light both candles with a match and then light the Florida Water. If you have never done this, you will have a beautiful, medium- to low-burning blue flame to work with.

Knock on the altar three times, calling out "Li Grand Zombi!" with each rap. Then, say the following:

Li Grand Zombi, I appeal to you

Li Grand Zombi, you are the father

Ye! Ye! Madame Marie Laveau!

I have taken this gris gris from the bayou

Come and empower it with your swamp magick!

Ashé ashé ashé!

Now, take your gris gris and pass it through the flames quickly so that it does not catch fire. Allow the flames to burn out and place the gris gris in the wooden box until ready to use.

BASIC GRIS GRIS RITUAL FOR HEALING

This is a very basic gris gris ritual for healing. It is good for mending a broken heart or helping to heal from grief of any kind. And it only requires four ingredients:

- Snakeskin

- 3 copper pennies

- Rose petals

- Lavender flowers

Wrap everything in a chamois cloth and place in a flannel or leather bag. Then say the following petition to Papa Legba (he is called Papa Labat/Lebat by older folks in New Orleans) to empower the bag:

Papa Labat, yay yay yay

Papa Labat, yay yay yay

Papa Labat, yay yay yay

Papa Labat, open the door and let the spirits through

Bless and empower this bag for your faithful servant

Bring him/her all good things in this life and in the life to come

In God's name

Ashé ashé ashé!

Touch the gris gris to the top of your head, your heart, then your mouth, kissing the bag.

BLOOD OF CHRIST GRIS GRIS BAG

This gris gris is based on ingredients listed in *Folk Beliefs of the Southern Negro* by Newbell Niles Puckett. I have augmented the three ingredients he provided with additional roots consistent with the purpose of the gris

gris, which is to "bring peace and safety" (Puckett 1926). To make this gris gris bag, you will need:

- Bloodroot
- St. John's Wort
- Devil's Shoestring
- Leaf and flower from a peace lily
- Sugar
- Spice
- Bluestone

Add the ingredients to a red flannel bag and recite the Anima Christi Prayer over the gris gris:

Soul of Christ, sanctify me;
Body of Christ, save me;
Blood of Christ, inebriate me;
Water from the side of Christ, wash me;
Passion of Christ, strengthen me;
O good Jesus hear me;
Within your wounds hide me;
separated from you, let me never be;
From the evil one protect me;
At the hour of my death, call me;
And close to you bid me; That with your saints,
I may be praising you forever and ever.
Amen.

EDIBLE LOVE GRIS GRIS

An edible love powder consists of ½ teaspoon sugar, 1 teaspoon peppermint, and 1 teaspoon grated candied orange peel. Mix a teaspoonful of this mixture in a glass of wine and the person will love you forever. So says Marie Laveau.

GRIS GRIS BAG FOR IMPROVING FINANCES

Marie Laveau was well known for using a variety of symbols and talismans in her gris gris bags. For this charm, draw the symbol shown in Figure 31

on a piece of brown paper. This symbol is the Andinkra symbol for good fortune and sanctity and was developed by Ashanti craftspeople of Ghana. Each symbol is associated with an African proverb, offering a glimpse into the cosmology and worldview of the Akan way of life. *Kerapa te se okera. Okyiri fi.* "Sanctity like a cat. Abhors filth."

Figure 31. African Andinkra symbol called Kareepa for good fortune and sanctity.

Carefully sew the drawing on a 4-inch piece of leather or chamois, design side up. With each stitch, say, "John over John." (This is an old Hoodoo practice that references the power of High John the Conqueror.) Sewing the symbol fixes it firmly in place so that it doesn't waiver. Likewise, your finances should improve steadily and never waiver. On top, place the following:

- A lodestone

- A small, fixed chicken wishbone

- Powdered High John the Conqueror root

- A piece of Devil's Shoestring root

- A black cat hair

- An alligator's tooth

To prepare the wishbone, clean and dry it, and wrap it in a yellow cloth along with a magnet for one full month outside by a gate. You may paint it with 18-carat gold paint for added power.

Anoint the additional contents with Louisiana Van Van Oil. Sew the bag together as a square toby. Carry it with you.

Figure 32. Altar of magick lamps by conjure woman Leila Marino of
Rain's Conjure Shop. *Courtesy of Leila Marino*

Magick Lamps

•••

A s much as Marie Laveau is associated with water, she should be associated equally with fire. She had a penchant for candles, incense, braziers, and bonfires, and according to oral tradition she also used magick lamps. Magick lamps are some of the easiest and most effective ways of creating change through supernatural means. They are one of the oldest types of works in New Orleans Voudou and Hoodoo.

Rootworkers use magick lamps because they produce quick results. This is because they are hotter than candles and can be mounted by the Spirits. Once you recite a saint's novena or utter the secret words of a spirit over a lit lamp, you draw that spirit down into the work.

When creating magick lamps, a variety of ingredients are placed inside before filling it with a carrier oil. The purpose of the lamp will dictate what goes inside. If you are creating a lamp for a particular spirit, you want to use items that are specific to that spirit. But, the first thing to consider is the type of container to use. Obviously, it must be fireproof. Hurricane lamps are part of every New Orleans household, so grab a lamp or two and keep some lamp oil and extra wicks on hand so you can work one when the need arises. Because hurricane lamps are built for heat, you can fill up the base with oils and herbs and whatever else you want to use in the work, put on the glass top, and everything is nice and safely contained. Here are a few more examples of containers that can be used for magick lamps:

- For a work of protection, use a hollowed-out pineapple with the barbs intact

- To petition Legba, use a coconut shell

- To petition Mami Wata, use a gourd or pumpkin bowl

- For general purposes, coffee cans, colorful ceramic bowls, clay bowls, and tin cans work

- For all works, use a hurricane lamp

Once you've decided on the container you will use, you then need to decide which type of oil to put in the lamp. Olive oil is a very good carrier oil for magick lamps and has been used for centuries for this purpose. If an olive oil lamp spills, for example, the flame typically just goes out, so it is preferred by many for this reason. Certain vegetable oils exude specific energies. For example, sesame oil, castor oil, and ghee (clarified butter) radiate positivity. Sometimes, oils are blended, such as olive oil and castor oil. Almond oil, corojo (palm oil), coconut oil, sunflower seed oil, and other vegetable oils may be used. You can experiment to see which you prefer, as it really boils down to personal preference. Of course, you can always use standard store-bought lamp oil, as it will be fixed anyway with herbs and other ingredients used for the working.

In New Orleans Voudou, special lamps may be dedicated to a guardian spirit. These lamps are prayed over and refilled with oil at the same time each day. This ensures that the flame will continue to burn until the petition is answered, and the desired goal has been attained. Sometimes these lamps are in fireproof bowls that are then set in a pan of water. The pan of water may contain offerings to the spirit of fruit and spices. Offerings may also be placed on a plate next to the lamp. Color-coded wicks may also coincide with the Voudou spirit for whom the lamp is dedicated:

- Black for Ellegua and Legba

- Red for Chango and Mami Wata

- White for Obàtálá and Marie Laveau

- Green for Ogun

- Blue for Yemaya

Hoodoo lamps are not typically dedicated to a spirit. Instead, they are constructed for a specific purpose. Offerings are not made to the lamp because the lamp is not inhabited by a spirit. Rather, the agency of the magick lies squarely with the conjure worker, as opposed to a loa or angel.

Wicks used for oil lamps will depend on the kind of lamp you use. Hurricane-style lamps have special wicks that can be purchased. If using a tuna can or clay or metal bowl, you can use a store-bought wick or make one from pure cotton balls. Unroll the cotton and twist it into a wick using the thumb and third finger (never use the index finger). Push the wick through a playing card or tin foil through which you have poked a hole. This keeps the wick floating above the oil.

Mechitas are premade wicks for small lamps and they come fifteen to a box with a floating triangular base with corks. It's worthwhile keeping a box of these on hand if you have a special affinity for lamp magick. I tend to keep a variety of different styles of wicks on hand for use at a moment's notice.

Now that you know the basics of magick lamps, here are directions for making and dedicating a magick lamp specifically for Marie Laveau.

A LAMP FOR MARIE LAVEAU

Magick lamps are great for a lot of different things but are especially suitable for developing a relationship with a spirit you are just getting to know. This approach is paramount to becoming a Laveau devotee. If you don't believe me, then go ahead and try asking Marie Laveau for a favor before getting to know her. You are likely to get smacked upside the head like Elmore Lee Banks did, because to her that would be a sign of disrespect. And she really doesn't like being disrespected.

When you create this lamp, it will not be for the purpose of asking her for anything; it will be an act of devotion and a means for getting better acquainted. It will give you a chance to show you are committed to her and are serious about walking the path of a Laveau devotee. Once a magick lamp is set on her altar, it should stay lit. If that is not possible, it should be snuffed out and relit at the same time each day.

You will prepare this lamp on her altar, so if you have not created an altar yet, that will be your first order of business. Then you will need a spot in the front and center to dedicate the lamp to her. The surface should be one on which you can draw her vévé (a blackboard surface is ideal so you can draw the vévé with blessed chalk). To do this, you need to draw her vévé and allow the lamp to burn on the vévé. This is referred to as dedicating the lamp "on the point" of Marie Laveau. The vévé serves as her calling card and the idea is to call her down into the lamp. She can only do this on her point; hence, setting the lamp on her vévé.

For this working, you will need the following items:

- Hurricane lamp and wick

- Lamp oil

- Magnolia bark for loyalty

- Lavender for blessing

- Jasmine for love and money

- Guinea peppers

- Snake sheds (do not use snakeskin)

- Marie Laveau Mardi Gras doubloon

- 1 white mustard seed for faith

- An anchor charm for hope

- Rose petals for charity

- 1 black-eyed pea for luck

- Piece of red brick for protection

- Feather from a mourning dove for peace

- Pinch of sand or seashell from the Gulf Coast[10]

The first order of business is finding a suitable hurricane lamp. You can buy a new one from a big-box store, or you may opt to look in secondhand stores for a nice vintage lamp. This lamp will be an investment in your spiritual life, so put some thought into it, but do not go beyond your means. We typically use hurricane lamps for petitioning Marie Laveau because they signify a connection to New Orleans, and by extension to the Voudou Queen.

Once you have found the perfect lamp, you will need to prepare it for use. The lamp needs to be blessed and dressed before you start. I clean my lamps with Florida Water first, then dress them with Marie Laveau's Voodoo Oil. After this is done, I hold the lamp up to my mouth and let my breath fill the lamp while I say Psalm 23 and ask Marie Laveau to bless and empower the lamp. Once this is done, the lamp is ready; it has been cleansed and blessed.

Next, draw Marie Laveau's vévé with blessed chalk on your prepared surface. Set the lamp on the surface. Add the listed ingredients. Remember that everything needs to be blessed before it is added to the lamp. I do this by lighting some incense and passing each ingredient through the smoke before placing it into my lamp.

Cover with lamp oil and light the lamp.

Light a separate white candle and set it in front of the lamp. Use a seven-day devotional candle as you will need to keep a white candle lit in front of the lamp for seven days. If the candle looks like it is going to burn out before the seven days, light another candle so there is a continuous fire before the lamp.

After lighting the lamp and candle, knock on the altar table three times and call out Marie Laveau's name three times. Then say, "*Mama Marie réchauffe ça. C'est l'amour, oui maman, c'est l'amour. Mama Marie réchauffe ça. Mama Marie, fais-le chaud.*" "Mama Marie warm that up. It's love, yes mom, it's love. Mama Marie warm that up. Mama Marie, make it hot."

Tend to the lamp daily, topping off the oil as needed. It's a good idea to keep fresh flowers on her altar. On the seventh day, thank her and provide her with special offerings of French pastries and anisette or champagne.

Once your lamp has been dedicated to the Voudou Queen, you can make requests using the lamp by adding a petition paper to the lamp oil. Be sure to snuff out the flame and relight for each new petition. Do not ask for more than one thing at a time. State your petition out loud followed by this: *"Bonne mère et bonne femme, prient pour moi."* ("Good mother and good woman, pray for me.") Always thank her and give her special offerings when she comes through and make a donation to charity in her name.

Supplications

...

The workings in this chapter come from Zora Neale Hurston's article *Hoodoo in America,* first published in 1931 in the *Journal of American Folklore 44* and later published in her seminal work, *Mules and Men,* in 1935. Referred to as the "Psalms of Voodoo" by Martha Ward due to their poetic nature, these supplications are said to have been passed down from Marie Laveau to those carrying on in her footsteps.

The Laveau supplications in *Hoodoo in America* were apparently reported to Hurston by two rootdoctors, Samuel Thompson and Albert Frechard—both of whom claimed to be the grandnephews of Marie Laveau. Whether or not they are actually related to Marie Laveau in some way is unknown, as Hurston reportedly used fictitious names, presumably in order to protect their identities (Hurston 1947). Of the supplications—or "routines," as Hurston refers to them—she had this to say:

> This is a ritual consisting of a series of formal petitions with answering directions from the god. . . I found them in Bogalusa, La., and again in Shreveport I discovered a doctor who depended to a large extent upon the traditional "works" of Marie Leveau. In fact, I came to know that practically all of the hoodoo doctors of Louisiana know the Leveau routines, though most of them have developed also techniques of their own (Hurston 1931).

Some of the Laveau supplications appear in the popular Hoodoo spellbook *Black and White Magic,* which is said to have been written by Marie Laveau. Published in the 1920s, *Black and White Magic* is a popular book that influenced the evolution of conjure throughout the 1900s. Since Marie was illiterate, she could not have authored the book. And, if she had written a book, it would have been in French. I suspect the book was written by Hurston—or its content was lifted from Hurston's work—although Long suggests it was written by the owner of the Cracker Jack Drugstore, where it was initially sold. She comes to this conclusion in part because of the products recommended in Marie Laveau's answers. Apparently, the products were among those sold at the drugstore. Despite the unknown origins of the book, it is a model for the kind of conjure Marie Laveau was known for.

The Laveau supplications follow a specific format. In general, supplications are a form of prayer whereby the petitioner kneels down and humbly requests assistance. A supplication always involves a request. The petitioner approaches Marie Laveau and makes a humble request regarding a need or desire. Marie Laveau then channels Spirit and responds with advice and guidance.

Note that if you read Hurston's work or *Black and White Magic*, you will see the supplicant appeals to Marie Laveau and a spirit of some sort, with the words *Goddess* or *God* used in the response. In the example that follows, I added Marie Laveau's name next to the Goddess designation for clarity. Note that in some editions of the *Black and White Magic* book, there is no mention of either supplicant or god. In her book *Voodoo Queen: The Spirited Lives of Marie Laveau*, Martha Ward identifies the answer to the supplications as being both Marie Laveau and the god or goddess mentioned.

THE GAMBLING HAND

Different versions of this working exist, depending on which source is referenced. The difference lies in the ingredients allegedly prescribed by Marie Laveau. This supplication is from Hurston's *Hoodoo in America*.

Supplicant: Great Goddess of Chance, I would ask your favor. I would ask for pieces of gold and pieces of silver from your hand for when I go to the racecourse the horse does not heed me or make efforts that I may be victor. And the driver of the chariot does not lash his steed that I may come in first line, but instead lags behind that I may lose my gold and silver. When I pray to you with the dice in my hand, you do not smile on me, neither do you guide the dice that they may show a smiling face to me; but instead you guide them that they may turn to the help of other players and I go home with my pockets empty and my heart heavy. So again when I set me down among the select men and play with them the game of cards, you do not put into my hand the card which will undo my opponents; but instead you put into my hand the low cards which will be my undoing and into the hands of the other players the high cards which will be my undoing. Tell me, O great Goddess of Chance, what can I do to appease your anger and win your approving smile; that I may wax fat and I may have into my purse the bright gold and jingling silver of the empire? I am your steadfast worshipper and would fain win your favor so that my horse will come to the victory line the first one, and so that the high cards shall burn to get in my hand, and so that the dice shall be friendly to me.

Marie Laveau (Goddess of Chance): My son, you have asked a great favor of me, but you have not burned any incense at my altar and have not made any offering to my spirit. For I look only on those who are my steadfast worshippers. For those who come for a day, I know them not, neither do I smile on them. [Interestingly, I learned this sentiment as well as a youngster regarding her disposition in reference to Marie Laveau servitude.] But for those who worship, I smile on them; for those of good spirit, I love them. So, if you wish to carry my favor, you will put into a small bag made of the *skin of chamois* the following holy articles: the *Grains of Paradise,* the powder of the root called *John the Conqueror,* the *powder of the*

Magnetic Stone, the *Eye of the Eagle,* the *tooth of a shark.* These you will close together tightly so that they cannot break out, and on the day you care to win, you will put on this bag the extract *Has-no-hanna* and keep it in your left hand pocket and let no one touch it except the money you will wager on the games, so that it will multiply and grow. And on your hands when you are playing with the dice and the cards you will put the *Essence of the Three Knaves and the Two Kings.* Pour of these essences in the palm of your hands and rub it dry and in your room you will burn the *incense and the spices of Saturn,* so that you will quickly get your wishes and the cards, the dice and the horses will break in your favor and do as you wish. But fail not to worship me and love me, for the day you cease to worship me will be your loss. And the day you cease to love me will be your doom, for all things I have given I will take away. For those who never cease to love, I am a true mistress and shower my favors on them; and for those who love me for a while and forsake me, I am a hard mistress and cause them deep sorrow and desolation. So Be It (Hurston 1931, 328–329).

The Gambling Hand Decoded

Some of the supplies listed in Marie Laveau's advice are obscure or go by different names than what we would normally recognize in a modern-day Hoodoo pharmacopeia. Big John the Conqueror, for example, refers to High John the Conqueror root; and Skin of Chamois is simply chamois leather, the kind you can find in any automotive parts store. The rest of the ingredients are described below.

GRAINS OF PARADISE

Grains of Paradise, also known as cardamom, Egyptian paradise seeds, Guinea pepper, and love pods, are best known as food for feeding the saints.

POWDER OF THE MAGNETIC STONE

This is simply magnetic sand or lodestone filings.

EYE OF THE EAGLE

I am uncertain as to what this ingredient is; it appears to be a curio with a name that is no longer used. As a result, I suggest using a cat's eye shell or omitting it altogether.

TOOTH OF A SHARK

This is quite simply a shark's tooth. Sharks' teeth are used for protection and can be placed in mojo bags or gris gris for that purpose. They can also add potency to any charm bag and can bring good luck with money.

EXTRACT OF HAS NO HANNA

Extract of Has No Hanna comes from the term "hasnuhana," another name for night-blooming jasmine (*Cestrum nocturnam*). Thus, the primary ingredient for the Has no Hanna formula is jasmine. Modern rootworkers often add a safety pin to their bottles of Has no Hanna, purportedly to make their luck stick.

ESSENCE OF THREE KNAVES AND THE TWO KINGS

Well known in commercial Hoodoo as a fragrance for gamblers, Three Jacks and a King is designed to attract luck, love, and an easy life. I suspect that Essence of Three Knaves and the Two Kings is a name chosen by a store owner for a similar product. I have not been able to locate a formula for Essence of Three Knaves and the Two Kings. The closest thing is Three Jacks and a King. One formula is as follows:

- Galangal
- Vetiver
- Thyme

- Patchouli

- Cardamom

- Cinnamon

Add the ingredients to a base oil fixed with vitamin E to prevent rancidity.

INCENSE AND SPICES OF SATURN

According to twentieth-century occultist Franz Bardon in *The Practice of Magical Evocation* (1967), the following herbs are associated with the planet Saturn:

- Black poppy seeds

- Willow leaves

- Rue leaves

- Fern

- Cumin

- Fennel seeds

To burn the above herbs as incense, simply blend equal parts together and burn on charcoal blocks.

Water Rituals

●●●

*"Li minuit tous monne a l'eau" [said Marie Laveau]—it's twelve o'clock, all
hands in the water—and everybody went into the lake, remaining
in the bath about half an hour.*

—BUFFALO EVENING POST, 1872

The belief in the sanctity of water is common throughout Africa, and
among the Yoruba it plays a central role in the creation stories. It is
believed the world was originally covered in water and that the first man
was created from water and clay. So central to the cosmology is water that
it is considered to be the most vital and sacred element of life.

Given the geographical location of New Orleans, it is no surprise that
Marie Laveau held many of her rituals near several bodies of water. The
swamps, bayous, Lake Pontchartrain, and Bayou St. John were frequently
reported as places where she held her ceremonies. There, she performed
baptisms and cleansings for healings and initiations.

The most popular of water rites in New Orleans Voudou is the spiritual
bath. Spiritual baths and cleansings in particular are a primary tool in New
Orleans Voudou. Most practitioners will prescribe a spiritual bath or a series
of spiritual baths prior to or after a conjure working. They are also effective
as stand-alone workings for removing obstacles, illness, crossings, and more.
Additionally, they can prime you for receiving all things good in life, and
attracting positive energies, love, good health, and rewarding employment.
Spiritual baths are typically made by the gallon from fresh herbs and botani-
cals at the time of need. Use spring water or distilled water for these baths.

MARIE LAVEAU CLEANSING RITUAL

To observe the Holy Day of Voodoo Ritual as an individual Laveau Voudou practitioner, perform the following cleansing ritual on St. John's Eve (June 23) or St. John's Day (June 24). This ritual may well bring on significant dreams that evening, perhaps ones that foretell the future, so pay attention to the dreamtime after administering the bath.

Take a soap bath or shower to get your body as clean as possible prior to performing this ritual. Also be sure your bed sheets are clean. For this ritual you will need:

- 3 white candles

- Incense

- White flowers

- Florida Water

- Coconut rum

Pick some music conducive to getting in a mesmerized state; something with heavy drums is appropriate, as are songs about Marie Laveau. I personally love a song by the *Dragon Ritual Drummers* called "Serpentine Seduction" for this purpose. However, I leave music choice up to you, as music affects people differently. What moves your soul may not move mine, so whatever it is, it should move you in spirit and connect you in feeling to the Voudou Queen.

Set up a mini altar to Marie Laveau on the edge of your bathtub using the aforementioned items. Line the three white candles along the edge of the tub. Light the incense. Set up the images where you can see them and place the offerings accordingly. Fill up your tub with warm water and pour an entire bottle of Florida Water in the tub. Pick off some of the white flower petals and throw them in the tub as well.

Stand naked in front of the tub and put your hands together in prayer. Say a heartfelt prayer to the Voudou Queen for what you need. Get in the middle of the tub and, while still standing, scoop up some water in the cup and pour it over your head seven times. If you want, you can lay in the tub for no more than thirty minutes and meditate or pray. Do not use soap. When you get out of the tub, wrap your head with a white headscarf and allow yourself to air dry. Dress in clean white clothes and sleep in clean white sheets. When you wake up in the morning, you should feel rested and renewed. As a gesture of gratitude for her help, donate to charity in Marie Laveau's name.

UNCROSSING BATH

This bath comes from a conjure woman named Madam Murray from Algiers, Louisiana. She was interviewed by Harry Middleton Hyatt, who stated she had been anointed as a worker by a Hoodoo Queen named Anna Pierre, who took up where Marie Laveau left off upon Marie's death. She offers a recipe for an uncrossing bath to deal with a legal case.

According to Madam Murray, the first thing you do when someone has been accused of a crime is give them three uncrossing baths. This cleansing process should begin three days before your court date. You take an uncrossing bath once per day.

Gather the following items:

- A bunch of parsley

- 1 teaspoon saltpeter

- 1–2 capfuls ammonia

- Rose oil

- White bowl

- Salt

Boil the parsley in a gallon of water for twenty to forty minutes. Allow it to cool a little, then add the saltpeter and ammonia. Madam Murray doesn't give a quantity, but keep in mind a little bit of ammonia goes a long way. I would recommend no more than a capful or two. Then, "Bathe from haid tub foot an' yo' don' put no soap." This is consistent with modern conjure practices for spiritual bathing. You always want to wash from head to toe to remove a condition and toe to head when drawing something to you. Never use soap, oils, or anything else while taking a spiritual bath unless it is specified.[11]

Next, Madam Murray says to put the salt in a bowl and add a couple drops of rose oil. Pray Psalm 7 three times over the rose salt, and then state your petition. Be as specific as possible regarding your situation, citing names of the judge, attorneys, and witnesses and how you want them to respond. At midnight on the third day of taking your uncrossing bath, take your underclothes and turn them inside out. That means bra, panties, undershirt—whatever underclothes you plan on wearing to court the following day. Sprinkle with the rose salt mixture and put them on inside out and sleep in them. The next day, put your clothes on over your underwear as usual and go to court. Your underclothes should remain on your person inside out. Madam Murray says, "Dat person will git a light sentence. Yo' sweeten up de names of de people—yo' don' worry so much about de people that's fightin' yo', yo' worry about de judge an' de lawyers an' yore witnesses, see cuz if yo' includes de people dar's fightin' yo', dey ain't nuthin. Dey don' mean nuthin. It is de witnesses an' de judge and de' lawyers dat counts" (Hyatt 1970, 2:1287).

CALINDA UNHEXING BATH

This working is from *The Life and Works of Marie Laveau* by Raul Canizares. This is a fine bath that is to be taken on Monday, Wednesday, and Friday for best results. As with so many other spellbooks, Canizares leaves out some important details, so I have filled in the blanks. For this bath you need the following ingredients:

- 1 head garlic
- 3 sage leaves
- Geranium water

- Dried basil

- 1 bunch parsley

- 1 teaspoon saltpeter

- Bay rum

- Vervain oil

- Honeysuckle oil

Combine the garlic, sage, basil, parsley, and saltpeter with a gallon of spring water and work the leaves with your fingers until the water starts to turn green. Add the entire gallon to a warm bath. Do not use soap when taking a spiritual bath. When you are done bathing, allow the water to drain, saving a cup to throw to the west at sunset. Rub your body down with bay rum, then vervain oil and honeysuckle oil. According to Canizares, "No evil thing can penetrate one who has bathed in the Calinda Unhexing Bath" (Canizares 2001, 33).

Figure 33. Marie Laveau altar showing Catholic elements and an oil burner.

Courtesy of author

Final Thoughts

●●●

In her lifetime, Marie Laveau practiced her magick on the bayous and swamps long since absorbed into the red bricks and concrete of the city limits. I have walked the same streets she walked, touched the same bodies of water she touched, breathed the same air she breathed, and performed rituals in secret on the bayous, just as she did more than one hundred and fifty years ago. I was raised and confirmed Catholic, just like Marie, and I have lit lamps and served the neediest members of my community. In short, I know what it means to live the life of a Laveau Voudouist because that's what I have done for my entire life.

Normally, when summing up a book you figure out a way to highlight all the key points you made up until the end. But that's not what is on my mind as I conclude this project. I have had many revelations about both the process of writing as well as about Marie Laveau the woman. I respected Marie Laveau long before I wrote this book. I knew the kind of woman she was and admired her from near and afar. But now, it feels like she is right here next to me all the time. I have learned so much more about her than I knew previously. In many ways, our lives intersect. In so many ways I can relate to her. In so many ways, I am amazed at the manner in which she was able to navigate the changing social conditions in which she lived. In so many ways, I am amazed.

For a number of reasons, it was really important to me to get this book "right." First, I did not want to contribute to a body of literature that simply perpetuated the Laveau legend. Secondly, it was important to me that I contributed to the greater portrait of Marie Laveau the woman, the human being. Primary for me was to fact-check everything I possibly could against the latest scholarly literature even though this book is written for a popular audience. I am fortunate in that I can do this because I traverse both worlds. There are those in academia who would not dare write a book for a popular audience, let alone write about Voudou as more than a participant observer. But as someone who knew Voudou before she knew school, it never bothered me to engage in the world of spirit at the same time as working in the world of science. Each felt as natural to me as the other. The problem came from others' discomfort with my reality. I have been met with bigotry, abuse, and projection for verbalizing my truth. Sadly, it seems the world has not changed much since Marie Laveau's day.

One of the revelations I had in the process of writing this book was the challenge of authenticating my content with sound sources. I quickly became aware of the irony—or perhaps even folly—of attempting to do so. I do not rely on websites and popularly sourced articles, although there are a few I may have pointed to. Most of my sources aside from interviews and narratives are academic. And therein lies a huge conundrum. Most of the scholarly information is written by people who have no clue about the topic they are writing. They interview people and base whole theses and dissertations on one or two interviews and on interpretations of others' interpretations about a tradition of which none are a part. Then, their work is published. And this is what everyone else seeking to have an academically sound paper cites. The whole process is a vicious cycle that is flawed from a cultural perspective as well as an academic one. Outsiders cannot legitimize indigenous cultures. Only we can do that. We must amplify our own legitimacy by placing the same amount of importance on anecdotal evidence and oral history as we do to others who are given greater status and weight because of a university or journal behind their name. When I saw one individual's dissertation refer to High John the Conqueror root as St. John the Conqueror, I knew we were more than in trouble. High John the Conqueror is a folk hero, a wily, enslaved man who was famous for outsmarting his master. There is a whole body of lore about this important cultural figure, including how he left his spirit in the root of *Ipomoea jalapa* before returning to Africa, so his power and gift of hope may be accessed by anyone in possession of the root. As stated by Zora Neale Hurston, "High John de Conquer went back to Africa, but he left his power here, and placed his American dwelling in the root of a certain plant. Only possess that root, and he can be summoned at any time." How does an academic get this basic, most important piece of African American folk culture so utterly wrong? I encountered example after example of this type of incorrect information in "sound" academic sources—scholars using Robert Tallant as a source without critical analysis, some claiming Marie Laveau was from Haiti, others claiming a lack of evidence for an African connection to New Orleans Voudou, and a shocking number using a major white Hoodoo marketeer to validate African and Creole traditions. It is simply mind-boggling the amount of "hooey"—as Carolyn Morrow Long puts it—that is out there about Marie Laveau and Voudou in general. It's no wonder there remains such a lack of understanding for African-derived and indigenous traditions. It's no wonder our story has been hijacked. Sloppy scholarship and institutionalized racism have contributed to this situation, and frankly, it needs to stop.

Before I decided to pursue graduate school, I experienced a similar dynamic in college. I specialized in Native American studies and was taught by white men who often got it wrong. And they really don't like being challenged about it, either! So, even as I tried, I was largely silenced by these professors who were more interested in being right than getting it right. That said, there were a few really good professors who understood the value and need for more indigenous voices in the world of academia. I was encouraged to pursue a master's degree and then a PhD because, as one mentor put it, "You won't be satisfied with just a master's." Another one pointed out that the ongoing colonial narratives will never change until there are as many indigenous scholars writing about our cultures as there are white folks doing it. So, I took the plunge. But our voices are still not loud enough. Our sources of indigenous knowledge are not valued as much as the white woman writing about a nonexistent St. John the Conqueror, the white man placing value on the interviewer's interpretation of their informant as opposed to the informant's voice, or the misinformed African American scholar citing a lack of an African connection to Voudou in New Orleans. Whether it is a lack of cultural competency or a lack of due diligence in scholarship, the struggle is real.

As Oya continued ripping the masks off the clueless during my process, Ogun cut through the rubbish, St. Anthony stood on his head, St. Maroon protected me, St. Peter handed over the keys, and Papa Legba opened the door to a reliable well of knowledge for me. Instead of using epic failures masquerading as scholarship for references, I relied even more on eyewitness accounts by clueless newspaper reporters—because at least they were providing firsthand, century-specific observations. In their fascination, othering, and propagandizing, they provided much-needed clues for linking Voudou practices from the century in which Marie was alive to the modern-day Laveau Voudou tradition. Narratives from the Louisiana Writers' Project, Hyatt, Hurston, and others provided the voices and opinions of the culture to become an important part of this work. Interviews with present-day practitioners and Queens lend further credence to the reclamation of Marie Laveau's narrative. And reliance upon the diligent fact-checking of Carolyn Morrow Long was indispensable in creating a cultural narrative that does not rely on scurrilous legends, but instead looks to facts to honor Marie Laveau's life and legacy.

Perhaps the most important lesson in my search for reliable material is that all fingers point to Self. I learned that I am the best primary source for my book, because I am writing about my own tradition and my own culture. Marie Laveau herself pointed out to me that my life experience is as meaningful as hers. I have something to offer to this discourse, something that is legitimate and valid. And just as she brushed aside criticisms and conflict, I can do the same.

Over half of this book did not get published due to contractual constraints. Some of the material will be in my next book, some of it will be used as material for my Marie Laveau course, and some will constitute a portion of my *Treatise on New Orleans Voudou*, a sorely needed work to fill a serious void. I realize more than ever the importance of writing down family traditions in a day and age where the information highway often leads to literary ghost towns.

I urge all of my readers to write down the folk practices of your elders while you still can. And to my readers who are fifty and up, write down your experiences—because you and your family traditions will be forgotten if you don't. I know that my own contribution would be lost to the sounds of frogs chirping in the Louisiana swamps had I not begun writing about it so many years ago. In the end, it doesn't matter that I was bullied and stalked and called a faker and a fraud for doing so. How would my haters know the truth? If they are not Louisiana born and catfish raised, how would they know? If they have never stepped into a swamp, played with wild snakes, and held séances on a Deep South bayou, how would they know? My contribution somehow threatens their narrative. Still, I take comfort in the emails and phone calls I have received in support of my work by people who also know but choose not to speak publicly. What happened to me is exactly why so many folks don't speak up and share. It is why—even after all these years—true New Orleans Voudou is an underground tradition. No one wants to be attacked and have their lives and careers ruined. There is still a stigma attached to Voudou, and there is still a threat when people of color claim their narratives.

Sisters and enlightened brothers, we have power in our voices, and collectively we are a force to be reckoned with. It is no longer acceptable to be silenced. Laveau Voudou is the tradition of Queens. When I am asked, What would Marie do? I say, About which issue? Being harassed and bullied for her beliefs? She fought back. Seeing undocumented immigrants? She was a stationmaster. Facing hungry children? She fed them. Helping people who are sick and dying? She nursed them. Assisting the homeless? She gave them shelter. Dealing with rape? She cursed the men and comforted the women. There is no one answer, yet the answer is clear. Marie did what was necessary to survive. She was not perfect, but she took action for as long as she could until her last days. She worked many different jobs to make ends meet, and she figured out how to make a living by identifying a demographic and marketing herself before doing so in the world of conjure was a thing. She was sought after, and her magick was valued. Her prayer was valued. She embraced her power in a society that did not value people of color save for their worth as a commodity. Yet, she excelled and became the most famous woman in antebellum New Orleans. And that's saying a whole lot about her as a living, breathing human being.

While this project is far from finished, this portion of it—this book—is at long last complete. I hope that my decision to explore the magick of Marie Laveau and her spiritual legacy contributes to a greater understanding about her and the religions and traditions she inspired in a positive and enduring way. This book will now become part of my legacy, forever intertwined with hers. As an artist, I see this book as one brushstroke in a portrait with many painters. As an author, I can't think of a better person to sit on a bookshelf with. As a proud Creole woman, I can't think of a better culture to represent. *Marie, ma bonne Mère, hâtez-vous de me secourir, prenez mon caeur et mon âme!* Marie, my good Mother, hurry to help me, take my heart and soul! Let's work together with Li Grand Zombi and make the world a better place with our gris gris!

NOTES

1. There were several women called Marie Laveau during the nineteenth and twentieth centuries. The Marie Laveau who is the focus of this book was reportedly born in 1801 and died in 1881. She is known as Marie Laveau I, or the Widow Paris. All mentions of Marie Laveau in this work refer to her unless otherwise specified.

2. I use the spelling "Voudou" throughout this manuscript to maintain consistency with the majority of the nineteenth-century sources used in my research. It is also used to distinguish it from Haitian Vodou, African Vodun, and tourist voodoo.

3. Marie Laveau's daughter, referred to as Marie Laveau II, was known as Marie Philomene Glapion, as well as Madame Legendre. The newspaper article cited referenced her as the latter.

4. From an interview by Michinard with Louisiana Works Progress Administration (WPA). Michinard. "Description of Marie Laveau and the Activities in Her Home According to a Niece of a Laveau Neighbor." *State Library of Louisiana,* n.d. *louisianadigitallibrary.org*

5. I have seen references in newspaper articles to this specific conjure doctor written in the late 1800s with three different spellings: *Clapion, Grapion,* and *Glapion.* I suspect the correct spelling of his name to be *Glapion,* which is the last name of the man Marie Laveau entered into a plaçage relationship with following the disappearance of her first husband, Jacques Paris.

6. The origin of Blessed Bucks is recounted on the website blessedbucks.com. I am not sure if this precedes the Hoodoo version or not but thought it a worthy mention, as the origin stories of so many practices are hard to come by.

7. The differences between Hoodoo and Voudou are delineated on a plaque hanging on the wall inside the New Orleans Voodoo Museum.

8. Many examples can be found of these practices throughout Hyatt's *Hoodoo-Conjuration-Witchcraft-Rootwork.*

9. Mississippi Death Conjure, Part 1: *youtube.com,* Mississippi Death Conjure, Part 2: *youtube.com.*

10. I realize some of these ingredients may be hard to come by. If so, you may contact me through my website, *creolemoon.com,* and I can help you procure these items.

11. See Denise M. Alvarado's *Anthology of Conjure Volume 1* (2017) page 28 for step-by-step instructions on how to take a spiritual bath.

REFERENCES

Alvarado, Denise. 2011. *The Voodoo Hoodoo Spellbook.* San Francisco: Weiser Books.

Alvarado, Denise. 2014. *The Conjurer's Guide to St. Expedite.* Prescott Valley, AZ: Creole Moon Publications.

Alvarado, Denise. 2017. *Denise M. Alvarado's Anthology of Conjure Vol 1.* Prescott Valley, AZ: Creole Moon Publications.

Anderson Jnr., George. 2015. "Fetish Priests/Priestesses Media Programmes: Examining Their Effects on the Youth in Ghana." *Journal of Philosophy, Culture and Religion* 9 (2015): 15–28.

Armitage, N. 2015. "European and African Figural Ritual Magic: The Beginnings of the Voodoo Doll Myth." In *The Materiality of Magic,* edited by C. Houlbrook and N. Armitage, 85–101. Oxford, UK: Oxbow Books.

Asbury, Herbert. 1936. *The French Quarter.* New York: Thunder's Mouth Press.

Bellegarde-Smith, Patrick. 2005. *Fragments of Bone: Neo-African Religions in a New World.* Urbana: University of Illinois Press.

Bilinsky, Stephanie. 2016. *The Voodoo Spiritual Temple: A Case Study of New Orleans' Spiritual Churches.* Arizona State University, PhD dissertation.

Breaux, Hazel. 1939. "Life History; Memories of Marie Laveau." *Louisiana Digital Library,* Louisiana Works Progress Administration (WPA), April 17, 1939.

Breaux, Hazel, and Mckinney, Robert. "Memories of Marie Laveau, New Orleans Voodoo Queen." State Library of Louisiana/Louisiana Works Progress Administration, 26 April, 1937.

Brown, Karen McCarthy. 1991. *Mama Lola: A Vodou Priestess in Brooklyn.* Berkeley, CA: University of California Press.

Buel, J. W. 1883. *Mysteries and Miseries of Americas Greatest Cities.* St. Louis: Historical Publishing Co.

Buffalo Enquirer. 1893. "A Voudou Case." June 23, 1893.

Cable, George W. 1886. "Creole Slave Songs." *Century Illustrated Monthly Magazine* 31, no. 6 (April 1886): 807–828.

Canizares, Raul. 2001. *The Life and Works of Marie Laveau.* New York: Original Publications.

Castellanos, Henry C. 1894. "The Parish Prison." *Times Democrat,* June 3, 1894.

Castellanos, Henry C. 1894. "The Voudous." *Times Democrat,* June 24, 1894.

The Colonial Williamsburg Foundation. 2019. "François Makandal." *slaveryandremembrance.org.*

Daily Independent. 1937. "Magic and Voodoo Still Rife in Louisiana." February 11, 1937.

Daily Delta (New Orleans, LA). 1850. "The Virgin of the Voudous." August 10, 1850.

Daily Picayune (New Orleans, LA). 1871. "The Condemned: The Decorations of the Altar." May 10, 1871.

Daily State Journal (Alexandria, VA). 1873. "No title." April 16, 1873.

Daily True Delta (New Orleans, LA). 1860. "Voudoo in New Orleans in Louisiana in 1860." October 21, 1860.

Davis, Matt. 2007. "Our Blessed Saint of Narcotics?" *Portland Mercury*, March 15, 2007. *www.portlandmercury.com.*

Davis, Wade. 1985. *The Serpent and the Rainbow: A Harvard Scientist's Astonishing Journey into the Secret Societies of Haitian Voodoo, Zombis, and Magic.* New York: Simon and Schuster.

Desmangles, Leslie G. 1990. "The Maroon Republics and Religious Diversity in Colonial Haiti." *Anthropos* 85, no. 4–6 (1990): 475–482.

Dillard Project / Federal Writer's Project. 1942. "Voodooism and Mumbo-Jumbo." In *The Negro in Louisiana*: unpublished manuscript, edited by Marcus Christian. University of New Orleans, 1942. *louisianadigitallibrary.org.*

Dillon, Catherine. 1940. "Voodoo" (unpublished manuscript). Works Progress Administration.

Eugene D. *Genovese, Roll, Jordan, Roll: The World the Slaves Made*, New York: Vintage Books, 1976.

Evans, Bill. 2004. "Tacky's Rebellion." *Jamaicans.com*.

Fandrich, Ina J. 2007. "Yorùbá Influences on Haitian Vodou and New Orleans Voodoo." *Journal of Black Studies* 37, no. 5 (May 2007): 775–791.

Fandrich, Ina Johanna. 2005. "The Birth of New Orleans' Voodoo Queen: A Long-Held Mystery Resolved." *Louisiana History: The Journal of the Louisiana Historical Association* 46, no. 3 (Summer 2005): 293–309.

Fandrich, Ina Johanna. 2005. *The Mysterious Voodoo Queen Marie Laveaux: A Study of Powerful Female Leadership in Nineteenth-Century New Orleans*. New York: Routledge.

Fett, Sharla M. 2002. *Working Cures: Healing, Health, and Power on Southern Slave Plantations*. Chapel Hill: University of North Carolina Press.

Fieldhouse, Paul. 1988. *Food & Nutrition: Customs & Culture*. Second Edition. Kent: Croom Helm.

Frieberg, Edna B. 1980. *Bayou St. John in Colonial Louisiana, 1699–1803*. New Orleans: Harvey Press.

Gandolfo, Charles. 1992. *Marie Laveau of New Orleans*. New Orleans, LA: New Orleans Historic Voodoo Museum.

Genovese, Eugene D. 1976. *Roll, Jordan, Roll: The World the Slaves Made*. New York: Vintage.

Glassman, Sallie Ann. 2000. *Vodou Visions: An Encounter with Divine Mystery*. New York: Villard.

Glover, Elmer. 2011. "Vaudou Practice in Haiti and New Orleans." New Orleans, Louisiana. Panel discussion.

Guynup, Sharon. 2004. "Haiti: Possessed by Voodoo." *National Geographic*, July 7, 2004. *news.nationalgeographic.com*.

Hall, Gwendolyn Midlo. 1992. *Africans in Colonial Louisiana*. Baton Rouge: Louisiana State University Press.

Hallam, Jennifer. 2004. "The Slave Experience: Men, Women and Gender." *Thirteen*, PBS. *www.thirteen.org*.

Hammond, Hilda Phelps. 1930. "Behind the Veil of Voodooism in America." *Dayton Daily News*, October 5, 1930.

Hearn, Lafcadio. 1886. "New Orleans Superstitions." *Harper's Weekly*, December 25, 1886.

Hiscox, Gardner D., ed. 1916. *Henley's Twentieth Century Formulas, Recipes and Processes.* New York: Norman W. Henley. Full text available at *archive.org/details/cu31924003643172/page/n6.*

"How to Conjure." 1899, *Journal of American Folklore* 12, no. 46 (July–September 1899): 229.

Hurston, Zora. 1931. "Hoodoo in America." *Journal of American Folklore* 44, no. 174 (October–December 1931), 317–417.

Hurston, Zora Neale. 1935. *Mules and Men.* New York: HarperCollins.

Hurston, Zora Neale. 1947. "Review of Robert Tallant's *Voodoo in New Orleans." Journal of American Folklore* 60, no. 238 (1947): 436–438.

Hyatt, Harry Middleton. 1970. *Hoodoo-Conjuration-Witchcraft-Rootwork: Beliefs Accepted by Many Negroes and White Persons These Being Orally Recorded Among Blacks and Whites.* 4 vols. Hannibal, MO: Western Pub.

Johnstown Weekly Democrat (Johnstown, PA). 1889. " A Voudou Sensation." July 26, 1889.

Long, Carolyn Morrow 2001. *Spiritual Merchants.* Knoxville: University of Tennessee Press.

Long, Carolyn Morrow. 2006. *A New Orleans Voudou Priestess: The Legend and Reality of Marie Laveau.* Gainesville: University of Florida.

Long, Carolyn Morrow. 2016. *Famille Vve Paris née Laveau: The Tomb of Marie Laveau in St. Louis Cemetery No. 1.* New Orleans, LA: Left Hand Press.

Long, Carolyn Morrow. 2017. "Marie Laveau." 64 Parishes. Last updated October 3, 2017. *64parishes.org.*

Manning, M. Chris. 2014. "The Material Culture of Ritual Concealments in the United States." *Historical Archaeology* 48, no. 3 (2014): 52–83. *www.jstor.org.*

Maranise, Anthony M. J. 2012. "Investigating the Syncretism of Catholicism and Voodoo in New Orleans." *Journal of Religion and Society* 14 (2012): 1–16.

Martinié, Louis. 2010. *A Priest's Head, a Drummer's Hand.* New Orleans: Left Hand Press.

McClean, James. 1949. "Voodoo at the Vanishing Point in Old New Orleans." *Sedalia Democrat* (Missouri), September 26, 1949.

McConnaughey, Janet. 2015. "Vandalism: No Solo Tourists in New Orleans' Oldest Cemetery." *Town Talk.* January 27, 2015. *www.thetowntalk.com.*

McKinney, Robert. n.d. "Description of a Hoodoo Opening Ceremony to Make a Person a Member of the Sect," State Library of Louisiana/ Louisiana Works Progress Administration.

Meridional (Abbeville, LA). 1885. Chronicling America: Historic American Newspapers. Lib. of Congress. March 21, 1885. *chroniclingamerica.loc.gov.*

Metreaux, Alfred. 1959. *Voodoo.* London: Sphere Books Limited.

Miami News. 1931. "The Burned Photo That Startled New Orleans with a Voodoo Mystery." June 28, 1931.

Miller, Robin. 1994. "Tales from the Crypt." *The Town Talk* (Alexandria, Louisiana). October 30, 1994.

Michinard, Henrietta. n.d. Interview with Martha Grey, Louisiana Writers' Project, folder 25.

New Orleans Daily Democrat. 1879. "A Voudou Maid Who Has Been Frightening a Whole Family by Her Vagaries." June 24, 1879. Chronicling America: Historic American Newspapers. Lib. of Congress. *chroniclingamerica.loc.gov.*

New Orleans Republican. 1870. (no title) July 10, 1870. Chronicling America: Historic American Newspapers. Lib. of Congress. *chroniclingamerica.loc.gov.*

Newell, W. W. 1889. "Reports of Voodoo Worship in Hayti and Louisiana." *The Journal of American Folklore* 2, no. 4 (January 1889): 41–47.

Oliver, Rev. C. A. 1885. "The Negro—How Can We Help Him?" *Catholic World* 42, no. 247 (October 1885): 85–90. *quod.lib.umich.edu.*

Osbey, Brenda Marie. 2011. "Why We Can't Talk to You about Voodoo." *Southern Literary Journal* 43, no. 2 (Spring 2011): 1–11. *www.jstor.org.*

Ouachita Telegraph. 1873. "Voudouism vs. Sickness in New Orleans." September 26, 1873.

Pensacola News Journal. 1936. "Voodoo Revival Seen in New Orleans." June 24, 1936.

Posey, Zoe. 1940. "Quest for Marie Laveau's Burial Place in New Orleans Louisiana." State Library of Louisiana/Louisiana Works Progress Administration, January 15, 1940.

Puckett, Newbell Niles. 1926. *Folk Beliefs of the Southern Negro.* Chapel Hill: University of North Carolina Press.

Rasmussen, Daniel. 2011. *American Uprising: The Untold Story of America's Largest Slave Revolt.* New York: Harper.

Reed, R. J. 1957. "Off the Cuff: Watch Out or Mumbo Jumbo Will Hoodoo You!" *Daily World* (Opelousas, LA). August 4, 1957.

"Remedy for Yellow Fever." 1853. *Scientific American* 8, no. 49 (August 1853): 392. *www.scientificamerican.com.*

The Republic. 1882. "The Fatal Sisters." April 21, 1882.

Richmond Daily Palladium. 1900. "Voodoo Queen." February 24, 1900.

Rigaud, Milo. 2001. *Secrets of Voodoo.* Translated by Robert B. Cross. San Francisco: City Lights.

Russell, Courtney. 2004. "Marabout Face." *World Magazine.* August 7, 2004. *world.wng.org.*

Salzman, Jack, David L. Smith, and Cornel West. 1996. *Encyclopedia of African-American Culture and History,* Vol. 3. Macmillan Library Reference.

St. Louis Post Dispatch. 1933. "When the Voodoo Queen Reigned in New Orleans." September 10, 1933.

Saunders, Steve. 2013. "Man Caught on Camera Dumping 'Symbolic' Pile of Dirt at Ralston Shop." FOX42, February 13, 2013. *fox42kptm.com.*

"St. Francis of Assisi." 1877. *Catholic World* 25, no. 145 (April 1877): 11–14.

Staunton Spectator and General Advertiser. 1881. "The Voudou Queen: The History of Marie Laveau." June 21, 1881.

Tallant, Robert. 1946. *Voodoo in New Orleans.* Gretna, LA: Pelican Publishing Company.

Times Democrat (New Orleans, LA). 1894. "The Voudous." June 24, 1894.

Times-Picayune (New Orleans, LA). 1895. "Mystery and Superstition." June 30, 1895.

Times Daily Picayune (New Orleans, LA). 1890. "Voudouism." June 22, 1890.

Times Picayune. (New Orleans, LA). 1886. "Flagitious Fiction. Cable's Romance about Marie Laveau and the Voudous." April 11, 1886.

Zogbé, Mama. n.d. "Interview with Mama Zogbé: Hoodoo: The Magic of the Afro-Diaspora." *www.mamiwata.com*.